Empath's Emotional Intelligence Guide

How Sensitive People Can Build
Emotional Resilience, Be Mentally
Strong and Build Better
Relationships

Mrs. Ashiya

© Copyright 2020 - All rights reserved.

The content contained within this book may not be reproduced, duplicated or transmitted without direct written permission from the author or the publisher.

Under no circumstances will any blame or legal responsibility be held against the publisher, or author, for any damages, reparation, or monetary loss due to the information contained within this book, either directly or indirectly.

Legal Notice:

This book is copyright protected. It is only for personal use. You cannot amend, distribute, sell, use, quote or paraphrase any part, or the content within this book, without the consent of the author or publisher.

Disclaimer Notice:

Please note the information contained within this document is for educational and entertainment purposes only. All effort has been executed to present accurate, up to date, reliable, complete information. No warranties of any kind are declared or implied. Readers acknowledge that the author is not engaged in the rendering of legal, financial, medical or professional advice. The content within this book has been derived from various sources. Please consult a licensed professional before attempting any techniques outlined in this book.

By reading this document, the reader agrees that under no circumstances is the author responsible for any losses, direct or indirect, that are incurred as a result of the use of the information contained within this document, including, but not limited to, errors, omissions, or inaccuracies.

Table of Contents

INTRODUCTION 1

CHAPTER 1: EMPATH EXPLAINED 7

CHAPTER 2: EMPATH'S EMOTIONAL INTELLIGENCE.............. 21

CHAPTER 3: BUILDING EMOTIONAL RESILIENCE 35

CHAPTER 4: MENTAL STRENGTH 48

CHAPTER 5: EMPATHS AND FRIENDSHIPS 62

CHAPTER 6: AN EMPATH IN LOVE 73

CHAPTER 7: EMPATHS AT WORK 84

CHAPTER 8: THE ROLLER COASTER 97

CHAPTER 9: SOOTHE YOUR BODY, MIND, & SOUL.............. 108

CHAPTER 10: THRIVE AS AN EMPATH................................. 120

CONCLUSION 133

REFERENCES 138

Introduction

"Sensitive people care when the world doesn't because we understand waiting to be rescued and no one shows up. We have rescued ourselves, so many times that we have become self-taught in the art of compassion for those forgotten."

- Shannon L. Alder

The other day I was told I am overly sensitive. It happened after I heard that a friend dropped their dog off at an animal shelter because their new landlord does not allow pets on the property. The poor puppy is being punished even though it did not do anything wrong. My friend had a tough time making this decision and it traumatized her greatly. I started to cry when my friend became emotional about losing her dog. The whole situation makes me sad. When I told my boyfriend about the situation and maybe adopting the dog, he told me I was being silly and should stop getting emotionally involved in these types of circumstances.

Have you ever been told you are 'too' sensitive or that your emotions are out of control? Yes? Then you might be an empath. An empath is someone who attracts both joy and stress into their lives through daily interactions with those around them.

Empaths share common experiences throughout their lives. We are highly sensitive beings who feel emotions deeply. Sometimes it is our own emotions and sometimes we experience the emotions of our friends or families. Some individuals describe this emotional affinity as being like a sponge because we absorb the feelings of fellow human beings. Unfortunately, this situation is not always great because some empaths feed on the negativity of others. It can lead to feeling upset or negative or even depression. Empaths should learn how to handle these emotions.

Empaths often cope with emotional baggage through time alone. Everybody needs time away from society, but empaths use this time to recharge and stabilize inner peace. Empaths find nature appealing when they require some peace. Animals especially play a big role for empaths. They turn to pets for comfort in difficult times. So even though empaths feel strongly, they have great coping mechanisms to continue their passions.

Famous Empaths

You are not alone in this world even if empaths often feel lonely. There are many examples of empaths throughout history. Mother Teresa lived frugally to ensure the well-being of many individuals in Calcutta while following strong Christian beliefs. Similarly, the Dalai Lama heads up Buddhism and strove to liberate humanity without any violence. Spiritual leaders often have a strong passion and intuition, which makes them empathetic characters.

Politicians may be empaths. A famous political empath is Nelson Mandela who fought for freedom from the apartheid regime in South Africa. Mandela endured great hardship as a child and suffered in prison for his political beliefs. His persistence paid off when South Africa saw an end to the freedom struggle in 1994. Barack Obama is another political empath that fought for all people to be equal. Obama often puts himself in the shoes of others and encourages society to do the same before passing judgment. A political agenda may be rooted in empathy and strong empaths can steer the political field with well-developed skills.

Empaths are found in the media industry too. The British author, George Orwell, saw colonial brutality while working as a police officer. His experiences led him to dress up as a vagrant and live on the streets to understand the people and what they go through better. As an empath, Orwell later wrote a book about his time on the streets and other books reveal additional injustices of society. Another empath is the actress Hilary Swank. Swank became a prevalent empath after starring in a 1999 film about a transgender person. Her role shed light on gender issues and Swank became a spokesperson for this cause. Empaths affect society greatly and can bring about change.

Many Roles for One Person

Empaths have many roles in society. Empaths are sometimes classified into certain categories based on their abilities. An empath may tune into the physical characteristics of a person like feeling pain when a friend has a headache. Other empaths pick up on the emotions of others whether it be happiness, sadness, or something in between. Oftentimes an emotional empath has a strong sense of intuition. They know what is going on—some people call it a gut feeling. Empaths that have vivid dreams may be able to interpret their meanings or even give insight into the dreams of other people. Empaths have a wide range of special abilities that some might consider to be superpowers.

Other empaths are categorized according to their attraction to nature. An empath with a "green thumb" often attunes to plants and takes great care that their plants flourish. Plant empaths value a fruit or vegetable garden and often live off their own produce. A greater focus is possible for earth empaths who consider the entire universe. These empaths can forecast natural disasters, weather, or other occurrences happening throughout the world. Of course, most empaths feel an affinity to animals. Empaths often have multiple pets and treat them equally to humans. Many nature empaths change their eating habits and become vegans to avoid animal cruelty. Any damage to fauna and flora hurts empaths a lot. Empaths touch every part of life and are very important for a balanced world.

What type of empath are you? Do you lean more to people or nature? There is no right or wrong type of empath. Every empath is unique in their own way. Knowing what type of empath you are makes it easier to use your gifts productively. It gives you a sense of purpose and belonging. But, you need to learn how to control your emotions to work for good. Empaths with high emotional intelligence have a big impact and live out their passion.

Expectations

Empaths are complicated individuals. We need guidance from time to time and this book intends to help you live a fuller life as an empath. After reading this book you should understand yourself better and have the tools to take control of your life. Building emotional resilience happens when you have the right strategies to deal with changing feelings. Once you manage your emotions, you can use your empath strengths in all your daily interactions. How will you achieve this confidence? Simply read the chapters in this book and apply the principles to your life.

Empaths have a strong sense of self. We will dive deeper into this knowledge and consider what empaths experience every day. Understanding your character and other empaths help in being a better person. It should help in identifying any shortcomings you may need to work on. Specifically, emotional intelligence is a term many people know and has exceptional importance to empaths. It is valuable to know how empaths exhibit emotional intelligence. There are both strengths and weaknesses to an empath's emotional intelligence.

Luckily, there are strategies to build your emotional intelligence further. Improving emotional intelligence assists in becoming mentally stronger. Empaths often have energy-draining experiences and you need to know how this affects your life. There are many ways to avoid falling prey to a negative mind. These emotions occur from many walks of life including friendships, romantic relationships, and in the workplace. Life is a roller coaster but empaths thrive in adversity. Are you ready to exploit your empath gifts?

Chapter 1:
Empath Explained

There are many tests on the internet that determine if you are an empath. If you are reading this book, then you probably already know the answer to whether you are an empath. But just to make sure, answer the following questions with a yes or no:

- Has someone said you are too emotional or sensitive?

- Do you feel sad when an acquaintance is sad?

- Do you celebrate when someone is happy?

- Do crowds drain your energy?

- Do you spend time away from others to recharge your energy?

- Have you engaged in negative activities (for example, binge eating or hurting yourself) when stressed?

- Are your relationships taking over your life?

- Do other people turn to you for your emotional support?

Now total up the 'yes' answers. Answering yes to less than three of the questions shows you have empathy but you are not necessarily an empath. If you have more than three yes answers, then you are an empath without a doubt. The more you answered yes too, the stronger your empath abilities. So how does your empathic ability affect your personality?

Empaths are phenomenal human beings. An empath understands the emotions of other people and tunes into these feelings so strongly that it affects their own lives. They are strong, compassionate, consider their impact on all aspects of life, and strive to make a difference. But empaths also have their problems. Empaths are emotional, tend to hide, and often disagree with others. Some people believe empaths have a paranormal gift due to their hypersensitivity to emotions. These things make empaths special.

A Day in the Life of an Empath

Every day is a new opportunity for an empath. Well-established empaths have set routines for emotional and physical well-being. You might not have this under control quite yet, but that is okay. Progress happens in small steps; you just need to start moving.

What happens during an empath's typical day?

An empath wakes up with positive or negative energy. Sometimes anxiety or depression creeps in and you dread the day ahead. Other times you may be ready for anything the world throws at you with overwhelming positivity. Morning yoga or meditation frequently appear on your calendar. It focuses your mind and emotions so that you are objective before starting on anything else. Many empaths set objectives for the day or make a to-do list to keep them on track.

Recharging at midday is crucial for your well-being. Empaths tend to use their lunchtimes to refocus their energy. You might go for a brisk walk, meditate a few minutes, or sit outside. The exposure to nature, even for just a short while, helps you to deal with the emotions you already experienced during the day. It gives you a better mental state. You probably spend part of or your entire midday break alone. You NEED this time away from the noise of other people's lives. Afterward, your colleagues may say you just disappeared, or they wanted to catch up with you during lunch but you were nowhere to be found.

As an empath, people turn to you for advice. They may come to you with relationship problems or ask you to do something that you feel is morally wrong. Unfortunately, empaths struggle to say no and often give in to the demands of others. You want to keep other people happy because it helps to make their day easier, even if it affects you negatively. Another people-problem that upsets you is dishonesty. Thanks to your intuition, you know exactly when someone is lying, and it hurts your feelings. You also refuse to lie to yourself. If something does not seem right in your life, then you will address it. Everything must remain in balance.

Getting home after work or school is something you look forward to. Your evening is often spent on focusing your mind to your empath nature. This time is your opportunity for creative release. Some empaths enjoy dancing, yoga, or other forms of exercise. Other empaths express themselves through painting, sculpture, or drawing. You might use this time to build something or spend time nurturing your plants and animals. Completing complex projects relieves boredom and gives you a sense of fulfillment. Your free time is valuable to you.

Empaths tend to avoid watching television or radio at night because violent scenes can be distressing. Yes, empaths even feel emotions without having a physical presence in the scene. Dramas, documentaries, and movies about murder are not on your watchlist. Watching the news is something you may avoid at all costs because it can drain you of all your energy. You would rather opt for listening to your favorite music or playing an instrument yourself.

Bedtime is your respite after a long day. Empaths that had a bad day filled with negativity might take this energy to bed. Unfortunately, negative energy can cause anxiety, nightmares, and lead to a restless night. Many empaths will journal before going to sleep to release any negativity and to find the positive in each day. Bedtime meditation, calming music, and praying to a higher power often eases the stresses of the day for an empath and leads to a better night's rest.

Some empaths prefer to sleep alone even when they have a partner. This situation is something that your other half may struggle with and you have probably disagreed about your sleeping arrangements in the past. You simply cannot sleep next to someone every night.

Being alone in bed gives you time to reflect and dream without any interruptions. A good night's sleep is something you cherish.

One thing all empaths have in common is tiredness. Empaths usually wake up tired, feel fatigued during the day, and are absolutely exhausted by the time they hit the bed. Absorbing emotions is tiresome and requires a lot of energy. Constantly battling your own emotions and navigating through the emotions of others during the day requires rest. The extensive amounts of rest and recharging sometimes create an impression of laziness to other people. Such impressions cause further stress and make sleeping properly an even bigger issue.

Empaths are creatures of habit. The daily events above shed light on the routine nature of sensitive individuals. Empaths need order to negotiate daily challenges and to maintain a positive attitude. Routines are the one constant in life that enables empaths to thrive rather than simply survive.

Signs You Are An Empath

Empaths share certain characteristics. These personality traits make empaths unique and provide them with their abilities. Some key traits give an idea of an empath's personality. Of course, not all of these things will apply to you, but you will find that many of them describe you as a person.

Exceptional Sensitivity

Empaths are highly sensitive to their surroundings. An empath will know about a small change very quickly whether it be an emotional or physical change. This extreme sensitivity to their environment enables empaths to understand the world better. Empaths often struggle with sensitivity because they do not have clear boundaries for their lives.

Intuition

Empaths know themselves very well. They are aware of every stirring in their body and often know more about their emotions than non-empaths will ever experience. An empath's intuition allows them to realize what will happen ahead of time. Some people call this a gut instinct and many empaths make decisions solely based on this belief because they know they are right. Empaths can use their intuition in good and bad situations. A bad feeling about another person alerts an empath to a potential energy-draining experience. An empath can then avoid this person and maintain a good emotional state.

Empaths are human lie detectors. Many empaths have a strong gut feel about people that lie. They can identify lies easily even if other people believe the story somebody tells. Empaths do not accept superficial answers. They have an inquisitive nature that makes them question the situation. An empath will search for real answers and only stop if their intuition is satisfied with the results.

Overwhelming Emotions

Sensing the emotions of other people can become too much. Empaths often cannot deal with turbulent situations and may even walk away to calm down. Celebratory happiness, extreme sadness, or traumatic events can push empaths over the edge. They are overstimulated with external events and struggle to process their feelings internally. Overwhelming emotion is the main thing that stops empaths from living life to the fullest. Only when an empath controls their emotions does the world become sensible again.

Daydreaming is one way that empaths deal with their emotions. Dreams create a perfect situation for an empath and help empaths to think about positive changes. Some people think empaths are absentminded or do not pay attention. This is not the case. Empaths simply withdraw into their own minds until the emotional chaos stops.

Introversion

Many empaths are introverts. They prefer to stay away from large gatherings because there are just too many emotions bouncing around. Empaths prefer to surround themselves with trusted family and good friends. Not all empaths exhibit introvert tendencies. Some empaths are quite happy to be around a lot of people for short amounts of time. Empaths also spend time on their own and are at peace with this decision.

Some empaths experience introversion to a lesser extent. Oftentimes, the level of introversion depends on the circumstances. An empath might be very shy the first time they are in a new setting, such as during the first weeks of school. Once they become comfortable within this new environment, empaths thrive and become less introverted since their surroundings are comforting. On the other hand, an empath that enjoyed their environment but now experiences tensions will close themselves off and become introverted.

Interpersonal Skills

Empaths are great with other people. An empath places someone else before themselves. They are selfless individuals who consider their own needs as secondary to other causes. Unfortunately, this selflessness can become detrimental to an empath's mental state.

Outsiders feel an attraction to empaths partly because empaths are skilled communicators. An empath has well-developed listening skills because they want to understand the situation in its entirety. This openness causes people to approach empaths for all kinds of discussions and advice. Empaths quickly develop a deep relationship with others. Some people are put off by the pace at which empaths move, which could lead to a breakdown in the relationship. When a bond breaks, an empath accepts it with difficulty.

Passionate

Empaths are passionate individuals that will fight for their cause and the needs of others. They throw their full weight behind fundraisers and other rallies. Even though they are introverted, they encourage other people to join them on their journey and explain why a specific cause is important to them. However, empaths remain behind the scenes since they do not want the spotlight on themselves.

Many empaths become servant leaders because of their passion for what is right. Serving other living things comes naturally to them and they will move out of their comfort zone to walk in the shoes of those around them. Their passion for the wellbeing of others is one of the few areas where empaths display less introversion. Your friends and family may be dismayed at this person that "we do not know" because they are not used to seeing you this way. Your passion is a beacon of hope for many people, so never dull the bright shining light emanating from your soul.

Commitment

Empaths are very loyal to themselves, other people, and the world as a whole. An empath will not let you down. Most empaths have specific dreams of what they want out of life. This motivation ignites a passionate route to achieving their goals.

Empaths understand when someone struggles. They know that life is tough and that every person has their own troubles. This knowledge creates greater commitment to other people. The problem with this loyalty is that empaths take on everyone else's emotional baggage. They will even forgive people repeatedly regardless of their bad behavior. Empaths always believe that the other person has greater needs, which is evident in their loyalty.

Nature Loving

Empaths feel at home in nature. Fresh air, the sound of the wind, raindrops on the skin, and picturesque landscapes appeal to the free spirit of empaths. Nature plays an important role for empaths—it is a therapy for the soul. Spending time in nature provides rejuvenation after an emotionally draining time.

Animals are a big part of an empath's life. Animals do not ask questions and provide emotional support to people. An empath will often turn to a pet for support and takes pride in caring for a vulnerable animal. Empaths are advocates against animal cruelty. They tend to take in lost pets until a suitable home can be found. The loving nature of pets is suited perfectly to the care given by empaths.

Self-Sufficiency

Empaths have an overwhelming number of gifts. Managing these abilities can be a challenge and an overwhelmed empath can lose control quickly. Luckily, empaths use their gifts to manage themselves in a positive way. Empaths take responsibility for their actions and do not shift blame.

Empaths know how to release emotional tensions. They have established daily routines that manage stress. Creativity is a major part of self-management. Empaths are artistic, musical, and enjoy exercise. Quiet time away from their busy lives is necessary, so empaths do not mind being alone. Many empaths schedule alone time to ensure they take care of their own needs too. Empaths are complex and unique individuals that make society a better place.

The Science Behind Empaths

As inquisitive human beings, we usually want to know why we act in certain ways. Scientists try to find reason in our emotions, actions, and specific behaviors. There are theories that explain some of the characteristics of empaths. Keep in mind that not all of these theories may apply to you.

Hyperactive Mirror Neurons

Neurons transfer information between brain cells. A mirror neuron creates similar emotions in a person when they see what someone or something else is going through. Compassion and empathy have a close relationship with mirror neurons. For example, when you see someone angry, this information is transmitted throughout the brain. As the message reaches your mirror neurons, your emotions change to feel anger or upset too.

Empaths have more mirror neurons in the brain than the average individual. The great number of mirror neurons make empaths quick to react to events. Brain communication between neurons is faster and more specific than in other people. This intense reaction often features compassion. You are placing yourself in the other person's shoes.

Sensory Processing Disorder

Something else that happens in the brains of empaths is sensory processing disorder. This condition complicates the way your brain processes information. The brain does not always know what to do with lots of information. We are exposed to many things every day—sounds, smells, colors. An empath can easily feel overwhelmed by their senses. An overwhelmed empath may start to feel anxious or struggle to concentrate. This reaction indicates that empaths struggle to process stressful situations. Empaths also sense emotions, and this creates even greater challenges in the brain.

Biological Sensitivities

The body contains chemicals and hormones that regulate our emotions and actions. Although any type of chemical imbalance can trigger empaths, the most well-known substance is dopamine. Dopamine is a hormone that conveys information in our brains; specifically, it provides reactions that relate to happiness and pleasure. The slightest change in dopamine levels can change your mood. Empaths are very sensitive and dopamine levels may be responsible for our quick emotional changes. Conversely, seeing other people happy or getting a hug can trigger the release of dopamine, which means our emotions and dopamine have a mutual relationship.

Electromagnetism

The brain and heart have many functions. Both of these organs emit an electromagnetic field that is unique for each person and depends on the situation. If we come into contact with another person's electromagnetic field, then we should come into contact with information about them. The electromagnetic field might give insight into emotions or desires. A furious person could have anger radiating from them–this negative energy is part of an electromagnetic field. Empaths are very sensitive to electromagnetic fields and receive lots of information when coming into contact with another person.

Contagious Emotions

Have you ever been around someone that is laughing uncontrollably? You just cannot help but smile or laugh as well. Other people's emotions are contagious. Empaths take on similar moods to people surrounding them. If someone laughs, an empath feels happy. If a person stresses, then an empath becomes on edge too. Emotions are partly contagious because of those mirror neurons in our brains. Remember that empaths have many mirror neurons, so you will catch feelings even faster than other people do. A strong empath can process these emotions to benefit everybody.

Chapter 2:
Empath's Emotional Intelligence

Empaths are highly sensitive individuals. Their personality and abilities give them a relatively high level of emotional intelligence. Emotional intelligence refers to your own emotion regulation and handling of other relationships. Empaths already do this quite well but getting to grips with emotional intelligence helps in being a better person.

Four Elements of Emotional Intelligence

Emotional intelligence is broken down into four pieces. Each element plays a specific role in creating and growing your emotional intelligence. Even though emotional intelligence is an internal and external factor, you can only improve your own emotional intelligence and that will reflect in your dealings with other people.

The realization that emotional intelligence is a personal characteristic is one that many empaths struggle with. Empaths want to change the behaviors and emotions of other people so that they live fuller, happier lives. But, it is impossible to change their emotional intelligence. You have to accept this fact. You might influence their emotional intelligence or set an example of how to be emotionally intelligent but you will never be able to overhaul their entire emotional intelligence system. Besides, focusing on your emotional intelligence makes you stronger emotionally and enables you to support people with weaker emotional intelligence.

Self-Awareness

Self-awareness is the foundation of emotional intelligence. It refers to conscious awareness of your own emotions. Are you happy, sad, angry, depressed, or excited? Knowing your own emotions creates self-awareness. Understanding your own emotions helps in expressing yourself and often improves intuitive abilities. All the other elements of emotional intelligence build onto self-awareness.

Empaths are particularly good at self-awareness. They know their emotional state very well at any time. An empath knows when they are on a high and can anticipate if they are sliding down a slope of negativity. Empaths frequently focus on their emotions by meditating or keeping a journal.

Self-Management

Acknowledging your emotions is one thing, but what are you doing with your emotions? You need to understand your emotion and then take action based on your beliefs. This practice is called self-management. It occurs when you productively take control of your emotions. A person with good emotional self-management recognizes their emotions, consider any hidden meanings, determine how their emotions affect outcomes, and only then choose the best course of action.

Self-management is a crucial element for empaths. The emotional storm can become too loud at times and make you feel overwhelmed. You need to take a step back and consider your feelings carefully when your emotions are chaotic. At this point, many empaths want solitude. Being alone allows you to analyze your emotions and get your head straight. You might realize that you were going to overreact or that responding quickly would not benefit anyone. Write your thoughts down in a journal and think about how it would affect yourself and other people. Many empaths use their creative time to process emotions.

Social Awareness

Now that you understand your own emotions, it is time to consider how your emotions affect other people. Social awareness helps a person to understand emotional displays by others. Oftentimes the specific environment affects a person's emotional response. Awareness of these factors also improves self-awareness because you may change your behavior to better fit the situation. You can use your intuition, verbal cues, and body language to be more aware of the emotional environment.

Social awareness comes naturally to empaths. You already absorb the emotions from other people through what they are saying or simply being in their company. Empaths have a specific problem with social awareness: a busy environment. You may become overwhelmed if the area has too many people, or if a lot of people are experiencing different emotions. You need to focus on the person or event you are dealing with and be fully aware of just the situation. Luckily, your gut feeling often sorts out social issues and assists in being more aware of your surroundings.

Relationship Management

Relationships do not just happen—they require effort and work. Relationship management happens through social interactions, communication, and responding to the other party's emotional needs. Empaths with high emotional intelligence identify good and bad relationships before approaching the other person. They know how to resolve conflict, what makes the other person happy, and often share an intimate bond. Empaths need to manage emotionally draining relationships and avoid toxic people. You should rather focus on positive relationships with a few close individuals.

Relationships can be challenging for empaths. Many empaths will have a lot of acquaintances but very few close friends because they struggle in relationships. The intensity displayed by empaths can be too much for other people to handle and they may back off. Some people have relationships with empaths simply to dump their emotional baggage. Be careful of these individuals because they take advantage of empaths. Trust your intuition when it comes to relationships.

Strengths of Emotionally Intelligent Empaths

Emotional intelligence is all about understanding your own emotions and the feelings of others that cross your path. An empath's natural emotional intelligence is a positive factor on its own. Your highly developed skills create several emotional strengths that you should be proud of.

Self-Awareness

An empath's greatest emotional strength is self-awareness. They are in tune with their own emotions. You know the difference between what you are feeling, and the emotions other people reflect on you. Empaths often build self-awareness by having a set of values, spiritual motives, or a life dream. You constantly measure your emotions against a benchmark set through these ideals.

An empath's self-awareness is a motivation for other people. Society will look to you as a role model for emotional change. Friends and family of empaths may ask empaths how they always pick up on what others are feeling. They could even ask empaths about emotional awareness and compliment you on your ability to express emotion. Even though self-awareness refers to you as a person, your awareness intuitively includes other people.

Compassion and Empathy

Empaths walk in the shoes of other people. They feel the pain of someone's broken heart and experience the difficulties of oppression even if they are not physically in this position. The intuition and understanding of other people's emotions create empathy. Empaths are compassionate and want to share the burden. They will fight for the right things.

Compassion and empathy only occur if you have emotional intelligence. It requires social awareness and self-management. Empaths first experience the situation and determine how they feel about it. They manage their emotions to portray compassion after understanding all sides of the story. An empathetic nature often attracts other people to empaths because they do not feel they are being judged or told off.

Listening Skills

A person has to listen well if they want to fully understand the situation. Empaths always have the time to listen to other people. They pay attention to a person's choice of words, tone of voice, and body language. Empaths also pick up on other emotional cues. Active listening helps empaths to communicate better and disrupts superficial conversations. An empath with well-developed emotional intelligence knows when they are being taken advantage of and will not listen to the stories of energy 'vampires.' This skill directly relates to social awareness and managing relationships.

Listening skills make an empath approachable and improve emotional intelligence. An empath's ability to listen well influences people positively. Your emotional intelligence improves if you remain calm while listening to others. Listening gives an opportunity for empaths to make a difference.

Self-Care

Empaths with high emotional intelligence know that self-care is important. Looking after your own body is crucial as it makes you feel good about yourself. This positivity creates mental awareness, boosts your self-confidence, and improves your emotions. Your emotional health often ties to your physical health. Empaths find a balance between mental and physical health through set self-care routines.

Empaths know that other people can overwhelm their emotions. Emotionally intelligent empaths take time out to look after their physical and mental health. They exercise frequently, eat healthy foods, and rebalance their minds through meditation or artistic expression. Your strong ability to look after yourself allows you to focus on other people too, which is what you want to do.

Future-Focus

Empaths are driven by the future. Emotional intelligence requires you to think about the consequences of acting on your emotions. This habit is something that all empaths do often. Some empaths will toil with decisions for many days to ensure they do not make a similar mistake in the future. Many empaths will think about their actions extensively before responding to another person's problem. They do not want to make a mistake.

An empath's "gut feel" usually helps in making decisions and giving advice to friends or family. Your intuition is a big advantage because you can predict future behaviors and avoid them before the incident happens. Empaths want their actions to make a positive impact on greater society. All the components of emotional intelligence are active when you think of the future.

Weaknesses of Emotionally Intelligent Empaths

Empaths have weaknesses too. Being aware of these limitations can help you to overcome them. Weaknesses are an opportunity for personal growth.

Giving In

Empaths easily give in to other people because of their caring nature. Oftentimes, empaths are an emotional crutch but forget about their own emotions. They fall prey to friends, family, colleagues, and even strangers who exploit them. Empaths with high emotional intelligence become victims of manipulation, but also give in to people without manipulative tendencies.

An empath's greatest weakness is their emotions. You already know that your emotions can be all over the place, which causes overwhelming emotions. Empaths tend to give other people what they want because they do not want to deal with a big range of emotions. A lack of assertiveness becomes problematic for empaths and can dent emotional intelligence.

Difficulty with Negative Criticism

Empaths struggle with negative feedback. It is difficult for them to accept criticism and to give criticism to others. Remember that empaths want things to remain the same and do not want to rock the boat. This situation makes it challenging for empaths as criticism is necessary for people to grow emotionally.

Negative feedback is always a touchy subject and empaths feel these emotions even more. An empath often experiences misunderstandings during social interactions, which can upset them quickly. This situation makes it difficult for people to approach empaths with feedback as they do not know how the person will respond. Likewise, an empath that has to give negative criticism feels bad for the other person and does not intend to cause any harm.

Rushing to Conclusions

Empaths use their intuition to quickly make decisions. Many people turn to empaths for opinions or a sympathetic ear as they know an empath will give valuable input. Although empaths consider the emotions of this person, they often forget about the effect events can have on others. An empath often gives an answer based on gut feel and does not think of other factors or alternative solutions.

Empaths do not want to hurt other people. They will select the option that creates happiness for a person. Empaths feed on happiness and avoid negativity, which often results from making unpopular decisions. Empaths could benefit from thinking logically along with using their intuition. Considering many perspectives can help an empath to make the best possible decision or give better advice. This strategy will improve your emotional intelligence as you think of all the options available and do not rush to the first available conclusion.

Decreases Creativity

Some individuals with high emotional intelligence have less creativity. Higher emotional intelligence requires the management of emotions and logical thinking.

Unfortunately, this management can cause you to question whether you are spending your time well. Your creativity is one of your greatest attributes so you should not hide it. Empaths need to find a balance between emotional intelligence and creativity.

Empaths are often described as moody, impulsive, and excitable. These characteristics do not align well with emotional intelligence. Emotionally intelligent empaths can benefit from structured routines. A daily routine helps to manage emotions. You can still express yourself but have scheduled times to take a break. Exercise, time for creative hobbies, and good decision-making can co-exist in the same daily patterns. Using routines encourages both good emotional intelligence and empathic qualities.

Risk Aversion

Empaths avoid risk. Risky situations can become volatile and evoke overwhelming emotions for empaths. Risk can affect many people and empaths do not want to affect others negatively. So, empaths prefer to take the popular route and keep others happy. Creativity is one way that empaths can manage risk as it gives an outlet for pent-up emotions and difficult decisions.

Empaths do have some tendency for risky behavior. Intuition and quick decision-making are traits of empaths. These are also characteristics of individuals that take risks. An impulsive nature frequently forms part of risk-taking. Empaths may take impulsive risks if their gut feeling agrees that the risk is not a danger.

Exhibiting Emotional Intelligence

Emotional intelligence is a strength and weakness for empaths. You want to remain creative but also take responsible emotional decisions. There are many ways to improve your emotional intelligence. Every person is different and empaths react differently to emotionally-charged situations. An empath is quick to action but may regret their decisions at a later time. You might even question your behavior and realize you know better. You need to work on emotional growth continuously.

The first step for improved emotional intelligence is to identify your emotions and weaknesses. Self-awareness is a major part of emotional intelligence. Recognize what you are feeling and try to understand why these emotions appear. Think of events that cause you to stress or make you feel overwhelmed. How do you normally react? Would you change your reaction if you had a second chance? If you know there is a better response, then you are already growing your emotional intelligence. You may realize that you need to take a step back when you are in a difficult situation. Evaluate your emotions before you respond. Your reaction to challenging events may change drastically and improve responses in the future.

Empaths are great with other people. So, why not get others to help you? Your friends, family, and colleagues may have perceptions of you that you are not even aware of. Ask your peers how they see you. Ask for feedback on how you react in good times, bad times, or stressful situations. Getting input from others will help you to see where your weaknesses are and identify your emotional strengths.

Keep in mind that feedback may have negative aspects. A person may say something that hurts you. The feedback situation is an ideal time to practice your emotional intelligence. Take a moment to think about what the person is saying without any impulsive responses. Use your strength in listening to deal with the criticism and decide how to change your behavior. Remember to keep an open attitude and neutral emotions throughout this interaction. Practice self-awareness and manage your emotions.

Another way to increase your emotional intelligence is by considering many perspectives. As an empath, you already walk in the shoes of others. But sometimes, we become biased towards an antagonist. You need to think of everyone's point of view. A friend that cries because of a break-up inspires empathy in you, and so, to you, their partner becomes the 'bad' person. This mentality causes bias towards the partner while your friend may also be to blame for the broken relationship. Placing yourself in the role of all parties helps you to be objective and control your emotions. Your emotional intelligence improves and others see you as a fair person.

Emotional intelligence requires a careful balancing of concerns and emotions. Even though you control your own level of emotional intelligence, you still have to be aware of the situation around you. Good emotional intelligence is something that many empaths struggle with for this exact reason. They place other people's needs above their own, which tips the scales of justice and catapults you to the bottom.

Get back up and become aware of your emotions! When your own emotions hit rock bottom, it is difficult to rebalance the scale. You may experience feelings of depression or that you are neglecting the people who trust you. There is no way you can live out your passionate care when your own emotional intelligence is suffering. Reevaluate the situation, focus on the emotions you are experiencing, and take decisive action to get back on your feet. Once you realize that your level of emotional intelligence affects your behavior, then you can affect change in the world. Every situation is an opportunity for growth, so grab it with both hands!

Chapter 3:
Building Emotional Resilience

Think back to your childhood and your first bicycle. Learning to ride a bicycle can be difficult. You need to learn how to steer, pedal, and find your balance. Sometimes you would fall off the bicycle. Falling off your bicycle could hurt–you might get some cuts or scrapes. Sometimes you would wipe off the dirt and other times a plaster would do the trick. But after every fall you would get back on your bicycle. Maybe not immediately, but eventually you would take your bicycle back out for a ride in the sun.

Life is full of tough times. It is a lot like riding your bicycle. Everything does not always go to plan and sometimes happiness disappears for a while. It feels like you are falling and can be painful. During these times you need emotional resilience. The word 'resilience' means flexing or reaction. Emotional resilience is about how you "bounce back" after an emotional setback.

Emotional resilience is something you build with time. You have to get hurt to build your emotional resilience. The more you are exposed to challenges, the better your emotional resilience becomes in the long-run. Emotional resilience requires self-compassion, mental decision-making to understand your emotions, and believing in yourself to overcome the situation.

Emotional resilience can be difficult for empaths because they experience emotion so deeply. Empaths struggle to get back on the bicycle after emotional trauma. Luckily, empaths can strengthen their emotional resilience by using their strengths in emotional intelligence.

Building Blocks of Emotional Resilience

Emotional resilience exists in every person. The level of emotional resilience in anybody depends on their upbringing, how they cope in difficult times, and their own motivation to improve their skills. Emotional resilience is a combination of three elements or building blocks. You may do well with one block but need to improve another.

The first building block is physical strength. You need to be able to pick yourself up after a fall. It requires energy to work through adversity. Individuals who are healthy and exercise frequently usually have better emotional resilience. They have coping strategies in place when their emotions get out of control. Empaths enjoy yoga and creative hobbies, which often helps in obtaining physical strength for emotional resilience.

The next building block is psychological. Your mental state affects emotional resilience. A person with high emotional resilience can adjust to different situations. They focus on having good self-confidence and pay attention to their self-esteem. Emotional resilience requires the ability to reason and think objectively. Self-awareness of your emotions is another mental element. Most empaths are well aware of their emotions but are careful of overthinking as it can break down your confidence. Empaths usually do well in understanding the psychological part of emotional resilience.

Social factors are the final building block for emotional resilience. Your romantic relationship, friendships, and family have an impact on your emotional resilience as you learn from interactions with them. Your schooling (previous or current), colleagues, and other people all teach you about responding to stressful situations. Emotional resilience makes it easier for you to identify problematic social interactions, avoid peer pressure, and improves communication.

Emotional Resilience is Important

Emotional resilience is important for all individuals who want a positive lifestyle. You probably already have several strengths of an emotionally resilient person. Empaths have some weaknesses that can interfere with emotional resilience and you need to address these issues.

A person with emotional resilience has self-awareness. They know their own emotions and understand their own potential. Emotional resilience allows you to accept a situation and find a way to solve the problem. Emotionally resilient individuals are open to change and consider all sides before making a decision. They communicate well with others, which creates solid relationships and enables them to resolve conflict amicably. Appropriate self-expression exists with greater emotional resilience and the person does not avoid challenging situations. An emotionally resilient person reacts appropriately and learns from the situation.

Empaths have good self-awareness and want to find solutions. They are strong listeners but may avoid confrontation. Empaths often express themselves in outbursts and struggle to contain emotions. An empath who wants to build emotional resilience often focuses on being heard properly, accepts all emotions, and does not harbor bad feelings after a stressful event.

An emotionally resilient person is persistent. Any individual that does well emotionally is aware of their own emotions and wants to understand why they react in a specific way. This ability enables emotional growth. You can overcome any situation because you know how to deal with your emotions. Emotional resilience creates perseverance and a commitment to improving your self-worth. This perseverance makes it easier to have relationships without fear of emotional outbursts. It also creates rational thinking and optimism in your daily life.

Stress is a major issue that affects emotional resilience. We are surrounded by stressful circumstances every day. There are work deadlines, friction with other people, financial concerns, or even just a traffic jam. All of these things can make you emotional. But how will you react? Are you going to give in, or will you bounce back and make the best of the situation? Having emotional resilience allows you to cope with different stressors making it a very important part of your life.

Resilience Theories

Many researchers conduct studies on the importance of resilience for individual wellbeing. The people involved in this research include sociologists, psychologists, neuroscientists, and many other parties who want to understand resilience. From the research, all theorists agree that stress is the underlying cause of a breakdown in emotional resilience. Stress management is the main objective of most resilience-building strategies. Yet, understanding the link between emotional resilience and stress better may give you more insight into the problem and potential solution.

Researchers proposed several resilience theories. Ungar's Theory explains seven factors or "tensions of resilience" that affect people daily. These seven tensions are material resources, relationships, identity, autonomy and control, social justice, cultural conformity, and cohesion. When any of these factors cause tension, a person's resilience is put to the test. No matter what your culture, these pressures exist and may affect your emotional resilience. Werner's Theory adds to these tensions by considering the link between resilience and age. Resilience improves as a person becomes older and understands their environment better. Unfortunately, some environmental pressures become too much and a person's emotional resilience may suffer as a result.

Another resilience theory is Rutter's theory. After conducting decades of resilience research, Rutter found that stress can have a positive or negative impact on resilience. Some stress is good and reacting to it builds emotional resilience and emotional intelligence. Toxic stress is the bad kind, which chips away at resilience. Even a brief stressful period like illness or trauma from an accident may be toxic to a vulnerable person. As an empath, being aware of these stressors is important because you are a sensitive being. Luckily, there are many ways to improve your resilience.

Skills for Emotional Resilience

Many skills affect emotional resilience. The idea behind emotional resilience is that you think about your emotions in a certain way, you perceive and analyze events, and respond in the best way possible. Dr. Harry Barry classifies these skills into three types of skills: personal, social, and life skills (2020).

Personal Skills

Emotional resilience requires you to have well-developed personal skills. These skills are part of your life and define you as a person. Accepting yourself, self-confidence, thinking patterns, and managing stress are all part of these skills. Your personal skills help in controlling your behavior and mental state. Individuals with good personal skills solve problems easily, avoid procrastination, and have internal motivation.

Sensitive individuals struggle with some of these personal skills. A person with low self-esteem or a lack of motivation often becomes depressed. High-stress levels decrease productivity and make people anxious. Individuals with personality problems must work on their personal skills to improve their emotional state. Empaths who accept their personality are more emotionally resilient.

Social Skills

Any social setting requires specific skills. Social skills help with starting and continuing successful relationships. The way you communicate with others, empathy, compassion, and active listening are just some of the skills necessary during social interactions. Emotionally resilient individuals make eye contact with others, are team players, and adjust to all types of social interactions.

Body language says a lot in social encounters. You can tell immediately if someone is angry, happy, open, or defensive just by looking at visual cues. A person that smiles is friendly while a frown shows unhappiness or frustration. Sometimes people cross their arms to defend themselves or turn their bodies away from a conversation when they need an escape. These are all body language cues that sensitive people pick up on and exhibit. Some individuals need to work on body language because they want to take part in a conversation but their visual cues do not say the same thing.

Social anxiety happens when a person struggles with interpersonal relationships. You might feel nervous, or struggle to chat with others. Some people experience this anxiety more than the next person and dominant individuals will often overpower conversation. Stage fright, reluctance to participate, and sticking to the outside of a social circle are all signs that your social skills need improvement.

Life Skills

All our skills together create life skills. They are a mix of personal and social skills, combined with mental function. Life skills include your ability to cope with stress, manage anxiety, and resolve conflicts amicably. Ultimately, your life skills help you to lead a balanced life. Solid life skills create emotional resilience.

Self-acceptance is the biggest driver of life skills. A person that respects themselves will look after their emotional state and have self-compassion. In turn, your self-confidence increases and this reflects in your emotional resilience. Life skills motivate you to do your best every day, whether it be at work, home, or while out with friends. A major barrier to self-acceptance is procrastination or putting things off to do at a later date. When you procrastinate, you lack motivation and cannot meet your goals on-time. This creates a sense of failure and you start to reject your persona. Breaking yourself down about little things lowers your emotional resilience. It is much better to make small goals and be compassionate if you do not succeed.

Improving Your Emotional Resilience

Emotional resilience is so important that we just have to improve it. You may start riding a hand-me-down emotional bicycle and learn more about your emotions. As you get better at controlling your emotions, you improve your emotional resilience. Soon you will be riding a new bicycle and even upgrade to a competition bicycle. You want your emotional resilience to be strong and set an example for others. There are many ways to increase your emotional resilience but you have to work on it every day.

Positivity

Having a happy disposition is important for resilience. But what do you do if negative emotions surface? Think of the positive! Create your own happiness. If you feel bad about not getting a lot of work done, then change your mindset by telling yourself that you will do better the next day.

One great way to make yourself more positive is to think of three positive things for every negative thought you have. So if your negative thought is "I struggle to make friends," then three positive things could be "I am approachable," "I am a good listener," and "My friends enjoy my company." After a while, you will realize you are happier because you are reprogramming your brain to think positively.

Assertiveness

Communicating with other people improves your assertiveness. It allows you to build your self-confidence and make yourself heard. Be an active participant in conversations. Ask your friends and family for feedback and see negative criticism as a chance to improve yourself.

Sensitive people often struggle with assertiveness as they tend to shy away from confrontation. It is difficult but stop avoiding conversation. You can only build emotional resilience with experience–remember that you are learning. One of the best times to practice assertiveness is during team projects, group discussions, and debates. Share your opinion more often and explain to others why you feel this way.

Take a Break

Just breathe! Taking a deep breath can help you to calm your nerves and emotions. Deep breaths give more oxygen to your brain and make it easier to think logically. Take some time out when your emotions become overwhelming. You can try the four-count breathing technique. Breathe in for four seconds, hold your breath for four seconds, then exhale for four seconds. Do this several times.

Meditation is another way to break away from emotionally-charged situations. Mediating also focuses on breathing deeply and helps to get a peaceful mentality. Many people focus on the negative energy in their body during meditation and make a conscious effort to release tension in their body. This method helps to reduce negativity and rather emphasizes an open mind.

Nature is a great place for breaking away. Have a brisk walk outside or simply sit on a bench and appreciate your surroundings. Playing with animals, listening to the wind or birds, and experiencing running water all calm your emotions. All you need to do is think of something else than the problems on your mind.

Productive Time Out

Productivity improves your emotional resilience. Filling your free time with productive activities increases your self-confidence, reduces the risk of procrastination, and makes a person feel good. What are you passionate about? Find your passion and spend time exploring it. Read a book to broaden your knowledge. Invest in yourself by doing a short course or learning a new skill. You might enjoy baking or cultivating a garden

Exercise is another option for emotional resilience. Take time to exercise several times a week. Join a group class, go to the gym, or run on your own. Some people enjoy team sports for an extra dose of motivation and thrive on the positivity of others. One way to boost your emotional resilience is to start leading an exercise group or class. Teaching others increases your self-confidence and empowers other individuals. What a great way to spend your free time!

Balance Your Life

Ultimately, emotional resilience happens when you live a balanced lifestyle. You need to adjust your time and emotional capacity between work, family, and personal growth. Being grateful is the first step to positivity. Take a moment to look around and think of all the things you are lucky to have in your life. You might realize that you have more to be thankful for than you ever thought.

Many people struggle with balancing life. One way to help you manage better is through planning. Grab a calendar or weekly planner (even your diary will do). Think of all your current commitments and schedule these into your calendar. If you work from 09:00–17:00 then write that down. You know you cannot spend time on other things while you are at work. You might have an exercise class twice a week and you can put that into your planning. Schedule all of these events into your diary. Now look at the time remaining and decide what you need to spend time on for better balance. Schedule some 'me-time' or block out time for family. Stick to your planning but know that changes may happen.

Emotional resilience comes from identifying feelings and how they affect behavior. You need to recognize stressors in your life, have coping strategies, and avoid excessively stressful situations. Adapting to change and persevering through challenges improves your emotional resilience. Accept your behavior, identify how it causes additional problems, and work on changing these specific actions. Through compassion and social awareness, you can become a more resilient person.

Chapter 4:
Mental Strength

Mental strength is the ability to stick to your convictions and persevere no matter what. It requires both emotional intelligence and resilience as you need to understand your emotions and bounce back from problems. Mental strength helps in many situations. One great example is a spelling bee. A child who is very intelligent at languages should be able to get more words correct but they might slip up and get scared. This fear causes even more mistakes as the child beats themselves up for not getting the word correct. Yet, another child may not do so well at languages but consistently practices spelling and has a commitment to improving. This child already overcomes mental obstacles and is likely to progress further in the competition. The first child has poor mental strength while the second child succeeds through mental toughness.

There are many examples of mentally tough individuals. Good athletes attend every practice and still participate in some way even if they have an injury. They support their team and motivate other members. Leaders also have greater mental strength. Leaders create goals, work towards a vision, and empower their followers. A personal issue or not meeting an objective does not derail a leader, but simply leads to an adjustment of the plans. Employees that are mentally tough consistently deliver quality work based on planned goals. Artists with mental strength can create masterpieces at all times and not only when the inspiration strikes.

Importance of Mental Strength

Emotional intelligence, resilience, and mental strength are companions. They are interlinked concepts; so, improving one strengthens the others. Improving your mental strength has many benefits. Increased mental strength provides better life satisfaction. Regulating your emotions becomes easier and you find yourself being forgiving and accepting towards yourself. This newfound acceptance enhances self-confidence and you start to actively seek new challenges in your life.

Managing your emotions and thoughts through mental strength enables productive behavior. Empaths with mental strength consistently find ways to improve their life. These improvements may include sticking to a routine, adding more exercise time, or learning a new skill. They know they have the ability to overcome any challenge or obstacle and refuse to back down when a small hiccup occurs. Mental strength might even expand your boundaries and decrease your introversion levels. Individuals with mental strength focus on the opportunity presented by every situation, rather than on their own shortcomings. This lust for life becomes apparent to the people around them and many empaths find great joy in the approval of others.

Mental strength builds resilience. You need resilience to cope with stress but you cannot do so if you do not believe in yourself. Mental strength gives you the confidence that you have the skills necessary to overcome adversity. Being aware of your emotions (emotional intelligence) and knowing how to deal with them (mental strength) improves your resilience. It allows you to get back up when you stumble. Mental strength is not something that just happens. You have to dedicate time and effort to it, so commit to building your mental strength starting today.

The Habits

Mental strength does not happen on its own. Individuals that are mentally strong exercise their minds often and adapt their lifestyles to boost mental health. They have set habits that improve their lives and prioritize certain behaviors that create positivity.

Positive Self-Image

Mental strength requires good emotional intelligence. If you can acknowledge your emotions, then it is possible to manage them and change your feelings. Any situation that pushes your buttons will require emotional intelligence and mental strength to conquer. Having good mental strength improves your self-confidence and you become in control of your life. Mentally strong individuals make a habit of identifying and analyzing their emotions before reacting to a situation. They know their actions and empathy affect other individuals but they accept that they can only control their own emotions.

Mental strength requires optimism regardless of your surroundings. The world is full of negativity, which can easily bring a person down. Mentally strong individuals acknowledge these negativities in life but do not let it get in their way, especially if they cannot control these events. Rather, a strong mentality allows you to pay attention to your dreams and put effort into building positivity.

Clear Boundaries

Setting boundaries is necessary for mental strength. Dealing with people happens daily, so mentally strong individuals know what they will accept from other people. They avoid toxic individuals because they do not want a negative encounter. If they have to deal with a toxic person, then they remain emotionally objective and deal with their feelings after the interaction.

Boundaries include saying no to unreasonable requests. Persons with high mental strength say no confidently even if it is difficult. They take responsibility for their decisions and refuse to apologize for unpopular decisions. They look after their mental health by taking on only what is possible and commit fully to these causes without it interfering with their positivity.

No Fear of change

Mentally strong people identify feelings of fear but do not let it overtake their lives. They know that taking risks can create opportunities for growth and help to reach goals. Yet, people with high mental strength know when the risk is too great. They take calculated risks rather than regretting a wasted opportunity.

Adapting to change and being flexible are characteristics of mental strength. Embracing change becomes a habit to become stronger. Many individuals identify a potential change and decide on how to approach it in the best way possible. They capitalize on good opportunities to develop their self-image, even if it pushes them out of their comfort zone.

Learn From Failure

Mental toughness happens when you accept your mistakes and failures. A person with mental strength will fail sometimes even when their mindset is positive and they are adaptable to change. It is a normal part of life and they accept it as such. They consider their failures carefully to identify opportunities for improvements. By making changes to their plans, they defeat their failures and achieve success.

Even though mentally strong individuals acknowledge failure, they do not let their mistakes undermine their positivity. They might feel down for a short time but then decide to move on. Any further thoughts on the mistake are positive attempts at improving their self-esteem. This approach builds up self-confidence and enables future openness to change.

Happiness

Strong people create their own happiness. They do not need other people to stay positive. They do not compare themselves to others because they know that this is only superficial happiness. It only causes resentment later on. Mental strength gives them the power to remain joyful and strive for better results.

Mental toughness does not stop individuals from celebrating the achievements of other people. They refrain from comparisons, do not judge, and understand that each person is unique. A mentally strong individual uses their energy to build up others and appreciate individuality.

Forgiveness

Other people may hurt a person. Mentally strong individuals still feel the pain of other people's actions. They use their emotional intelligence to understand their feelings about the negative situation. They also attempt to understand the social interaction from the other person's point of view. Mental strength stops a person from dwelling on the negative person.

Mentally strong people forgive others when they make a mistake. They know that holding onto negative emotions creates unnecessary stress and dampens an optimistic mindset. Besides, they cannot change the other person's actions and they also do not need to accept the behavior. Forgiving someone frees your mind to focus on your priorities rather than stewing in someone else's poor choices.

Self-Care

Strong mentality comes from looking after yourself. People with high mental strength exercise often to release endorphins and improve their confidence. This happiness makes it easier to deal with tough situations. They also get enough sleep. A good night's sleep gives your mind time to rest and removes toxins from your body. It makes their memory better and gives them the ability to work through their emotions.

Another part of their self-care routine is consuming healthy foods. Mentally strong individuals eat lots of fruit and vegetables. It gives them the necessary vitamins and minerals to think clearly and balance the chemicals in the body. They avoid caffeine–coffee, energy drinks, and fizzy beverages. Too much caffeine creates hyperactive emotions, which makes it difficult to react logically in troubling situations. Mentally strong people use their positivity and other strategies to increase their energy. They do not rely on artificial substances.

A Mental Workout

Mental strength can be built just like you would exercise for physical strength. A mental workout only takes a few minutes per day. After a while, you will realize that your mental exercise has become continuous and you now practice it several times throughout the day.

Set Goals

Start your work out by setting goals. They do not have to be big goals. It is perfectly fine to start with small, attainable goals. What area of your life do you want to work on? Make a quick list of these things and choose one to focus on at a time. Maybe you want to exercise more, so your goal could be to exercise twice every week. Some people want to eat more healthily and may set a goal of not eating sugar for 3 days. If you do not socialize often, then decide to call a friend every Sunday for a month. These small goals are easy to achieve and create a positive mindset.

Celebrate Small Wins

Have you reached your goal? Great! Let's celebrate! Reward yourself for your achievements. After eating healthy all week you could treat yourself to ice cream on the weekend. Or maybe you buy the shirt you have had your eye on after exercising all month. Some people like to decide on a reward when they set their goals. It gives you a chance to meet your goals and get a reward for working hard. Remember to share your achievements with the important people in your life as they also want to celebrate with you, which gives another mental boost.

Create Boundaries

Highly sensitive individuals often struggle with setting boundaries. You need to overcome this problem. Stop saying yes to everything or giving in to the requests of others. You cannot keep everybody happy. Stay away from people who often ask you for things. You should protect your mental health, money, and time. Working unpaid extra hours because your boss asks you to is not something you have to do. Say no to your friend who wants to borrow money if you cannot afford to help at the moment. Do not feel bad if you have to say no to people because you are protecting your mental strength.

Be Grateful

Mental strength increases when you are thankful. You should be grateful for everything in your life. Most people have a lot of things to be thankful for but take them for granted. Be grateful for nature–something that is so important to empaths. If you have food, family support, and a home, then you are already rich in life. Appreciate it! So next time you feel negative about something, think about what you have that others might not be lucky enough to possess.

Try and Try Again

Falling down or getting hurt mentally is inevitable. You will make mistakes but get up, dust yourself off, and move on. Mental strength builds when you overcome challenges. If your goal was to do 20 push-ups every day and you only manage 12 on the first day, then try again tomorrow. Do not give up. It is okay. If you can do 14 push-ups the next day then you have already improved your physical strength and mentally pushed yourself to do more. You can do whatever you set your mind to–just keep trying!

Commit to New Habits

Habits help you to stay motivated and reach goals. Exercising several times a week or reading every night are all habits. Try to create positive habits in your life. Again, start small. Maybe morning traffic stresses you out and overwhelms you for the first half of your workday. You could decide to leave home ten minutes earlier so that you arrive at work ten minutes earlier. Then you can take a quick walk or spend a few minutes taking deep breaths to refocus your mind and create a positive attitude. So your habit would be to leave ten minutes earlier and this small change can have a positive impact all day. Do not worry if you skip a day. Just get back onto your habit the next day.

Recharge

Taking time to reboot your mind and soul is important for mental strength. Your mind needs recovery time and the best way to rest is through looking after yourself. Sleep at least eight hours every night, eat healthy foods, and spend time alone. It gives your brain a rest from all the difficulties of life. Recharging gives you the ability to face challenges the next day and build mental muscles.

Avoid Mental Strength Pitfalls

Not every person has naturally strong mental health and even those who are mentally strong struggle from time to time. You need to overcome these circumstances to improve your mental strength. Noticing the warning signs can help you to stop yourself from slipping back. Sometimes you just need to focus on these problems before trying to take big leaps in mental exercise. It will already help to build your mental strength.

Stop Wasting Time and Energy

Wasting resources is a big problem when it comes to mental strength. We spend a lot of time fretting over silly things, procrastinating, and worrying ourselves sick. You need to stop this behavior if you want to strengthen your mind. Do not wallow in your self-pity when you do not succeed at something. Most of the things you stress about are out of your control, so wasting energy on worrying is unnecessary. You cannot control the traffic conditions when there is a car accident, so stop stressing about it. Rather, focus on how you can rearrange your day to make up for the lost time stuck in traffic. Accept the circumstances and make the best of it.

Uncontrollable Emotions

You can control your own emotions. You cannot control the emotions and behaviors of other people. Mental strength decreases when people are overwhelmed by emotions or have emotional outbursts. This behavior prevents mental strength. Start controlling your emotions if you want to improve your mental strength. At the same time, remember that you cannot control other people. They might react negatively to your decision-making or push for an action that you do not agree with. You can manage your response to these situations through emotional intelligence. Your logical and appropriate behavior might even highlight poor behavior by the other person. So, react appropriately, grow your mental strength, and effect change in others.

Avoid Repetitive Mistakes

Making mistakes can be embarrassing but they are part of life. A mentally weak person thinks about their mistakes often and may feel like a failure. This mindset is a major barrier to mental strength. Rather than feeling bad, think about what your mistake taught you. What can you do better next time? How would you change your actions or behavior after the mistake? Overcoming your mistakes and improving yourself are all parts of building mental strength. Just try not to make the same mistake again.

Fear and Change

Being scared to do something or not wanting to change stops you from building mental strength. Many individuals do not follow their dreams because they are scared of failure or embarrassment. They would rather sit back and let the world go by. Some people do not want to change at all, even if it will be a positive change. These things stop you from building your mental strength. You need to adjust to change and open yourself up to new opportunities. If you do fail, then chalk it up as a life lesson and move on.

Taking Responsibility

Mental weakness often comes across when people do not take responsibility for their own actions. They shift the blame to other people, struggle to admit their own faults, and envy the success of other people. These behaviors do not help your mind to become stronger. You need to accept that your decisions and actions will affect your present and future. Only you can create your own success regardless of your circumstances. Being mentally strong requires you to determine your own destiny and appreciate the success of your friends and family. Being accountable and celebrating achievements helps you to be positive and affects your mental health.

You are capable of improving your mental strength! Identify your behaviors and habits that decrease mental toughness. Work on these issues and know that you can succeed. You are the only person that can make a change to your mental state. Focus on your strengths and address your weaknesses. Reward yourself for reaching your targets and do not dwell on your failures.

Chapter 5:
Empaths and Friendships

Having friends is a blessing! They lighten up your life and improve your mental health. Friendships help us to manage stress and keep us accountable for our actions. Having friends makes us better human beings. Friendships are especially important for empaths because it is an opportunity to make a difference.

Good friends provide social support during tough times. They give a shoulder to cry on and celebrate the good times. Having positive friendships improves your self-esteem. Empaths need a few great friends to beat their loneliness and encourage them to use their gifts. Meeting new friends is an opportunity to learn an unknown skill, start a different hobby, and be more active in your community.

Significance of Friendships

All people seek companionship and friendship since it provides purpose to their lives. A mutual friendship has many advantages for empaths but we are reluctant to make friends. Allowing other people into your life can cause upset but the benefits far outweigh the potential consequences (if there are any at all).

Friendships require attention and time together so it is a chance to enhance your social skills. You can have fun together and laugh about silly things. This happiness releases the hormone dopamine and leaves you feeling content. Positive time spent with friends is a stress reliever too. As you share your worries, you start to relax and your body releases endorphins. This hormone reduces your stress level and increases your mental strength. Soon, you start feeling as if you can cope better.

Friends help you to blossom. A good friend should encourage you to become the best version of yourself. They support you in good and bad times. If your friend really cares, they will also call you out on incorrect behavior. Empaths often see this as a bad thing but you should use it as a growth opportunity. Your friend is looking out for you and has your best interests at heart. After all, your friend is presenting you with a real-life situation that requires emotional intelligence, resilience, and mental strength. It is the ideal opportunity to improve yourself in a safe environment. But, many empaths struggle with friendships.

Reluctant Participation

Making friends is not always easy, especially for empaths. The strong emotional connection that empaths have with people can scare possible friends away. Empaths are sometimes described as over-the-top in social settings, while they withdraw at other times. Not all people can handle these fluctuating emotions. These issues are challenging for empaths. Many highly sensitive individuals struggle with friendships because they need their time alone.

Sensing Emotions

Empaths have a natural affinity for others. An empath can walk into a room and immediately take on the main emotion. If everyone is happy, then an empath becomes happy. If someone is sad, then an empath becomes sad. These mood flips are not easy to handle. You may feel that you lose yourself in the chaos of all these emotions.

Imagine that you are at a busy restaurant having dinner with friends. You are all happy and laughing about a funny memory. Your friends are a positive influence in your life and things are good. As you look around the restaurant, you spot a parent scolding a child. You can feel the parent's rage in your being, even though you do not know what the child did wrong. At the same time, the child speaks to your soul as well. You feel sad for the child being told off and sense their defeat at being told off. These emotions distract you from your friends. Your mood might change to be more negative. Some of your friends may tell you to cheer up and others would not even notice that your attitude has changed. Talking to your friends about the parent and child at a later time will probably result in a frown. Your friends will forget about it right after it happened, but your mind will dwell on these emotions for several days.

Sensing emotions is a special gift. It is not something that everyone can do. You should feel grateful for this sensitivity, even if it is difficult at times. Embrace this gift but try to control it when you are at a social gathering. Stay in the moment and focus on your friends rather than concentrating on the emotions of strangers. If you do get distracted, then take some deep breaths and clear your mind. A great way to refocus is simply by asking your friend to repeat what they just said. You then have to concentrate on your friend's response and become part of the conversation once again.

Social Avoidance

The overwhelming emotional connection with people often makes empaths reluctant to take part in social settings. They tend to avoid get-togethers because they know there are too many feelings floating around. Staying away from parties allows empaths to remain in control of their lives. It is a strategy to stop negative emotions. These attacking emotions can stop you from meeting new people or building your friendships. You may decide not to approach any person at an event and stay in the corner or alone outside. The truth is that many people enjoy the company of empaths because they are vibrant, energetic, and care about other things than the norm. Isolating yourself is a defense mechanism but should not get in the way of spending time with others.

Your friends may have remarked on your absence from events. It is difficult to explain to people why you do not want to go for coffee or to a concert. Your senses are just too alert and overstimulation is not what you want at that moment. Empaths need their time away from other people.

Empaths use alone time to recharge. Too many emotions leave you feeling tired emotionally. You deplete your mental strength and need to build it up again. Many empaths worry about social interaction for a long time after leaving the event. They replay discussions and emotions over and over. You might want to make sense of what happened. Unfortunately, it is not always possible to find a reason, especially when it comes to other people. You might not understand why your friends acted in a certain way, but you need to realize that it is out of your control. You cannot take responsibility for their actions. So when you have your alone time, acknowledge your feelings about the situation then refocus on the positives of your friendship. Spend your time away doing positive things. Then you can go to your next social event feeling excited and upbeat about friendships.

Troublesome Friendships

Many people want empaths as friends because they are super reliable. Your friends know you are always there to listen to their problems. Unfortunately, this situation quickly leads to manipulative behavior. You need to identify troublesome friendships that threaten your emotional security as it will only bring you down while building the other person up.

Fixing People

Empaths often become friends that seem to be 'projects.' A project friend is someone who has turbulent emotions and seeks attention. Empaths feel they can fix these friends, but at what cost? You might want to heal your friends but your mental health will suffer.

Fixing people takes time and energy. Your friend might just have told you all about their work or romantic issues. It took more than an hour and you had other things to do like cooking, exercise, or even work. Now, you feel tired because of all this emotional baggage dumped onto you. You probably will not get to all your commitments and feel emotionally drained for days to come. Luckily for your friend, they feel emotionally uplifted and ready to face the world.

Your excellent listening skills are part of what draws people closer. But you need to learn how to control these encounters. Empaths should not be held hostage to their friend's emotions. Help your friends and be there for them but do not let it affect your emotional intelligence and mental strength. Protect your own emotions and lifestyle. You already have quite a few tools to cope with recharging and getting back on track.

Your Role as a Friend

People might treat you like one, but you are not a therapist. Spending time with friends should be a breakaway activity. It should not be all-consuming and something you dread. You have your own needs from friendships too. Your friend is not the only person who wants support. Choose friends that you can support positively while knowing that they have your back as well.

A great strategy for social encounters is to think about who you will see ahead of time. You know your friends and what their issues are, so avoid these topics at all costs. What are some of your friend's hobbies? What music do they like? Are they busy with an uplifting project? Ask your friends about these types of activities rather than discussing work or difficult romantic relationships.

One way to be available to your friends is to set clear boundaries for social encounters. You can prepare mentally for dinners or parties but do not let other interactions affect your day. Many empaths find phone calls a big issue. They cannot prepare for phone conversations as they happen impulsively. So if a friend does call you, then simply tell them that you only have two minutes before you need to hang up. Your friend will probably get right to the actual issue without all the other emotions in between. This strategy limits your involvement while still showing you care.

Encouragement

Friends are a source of encouragement. They are a pillar of support. You also play these roles in the lives of your friends. It is a reciprocal relationship that you should look after, especially if your friends take care of your emotions too. A great friendship will build up both of you but you need boundaries for that to happen.

Be open to your friends about your struggles as an empath. Explain your emotions to your friends. It gives them an opportunity to understand that you do want to help but cannot always be available emotionally. A true friend will accept these boundaries. In fact, they might even become the best mental health supporters.

Remember that your friends are not projects. They are human beings with their own unique needs just like yours. If you feel your friend is struggling with something, then direct them to a place that can help. You might suggest they visit a social worker, seek assistance from a non-profit company, or attend a therapy group. These ideas show your friends that you can care but that you cannot be a shoulder to cry on all the time.

It is absolutely fine to support your friends but know what behaviors you cannot accept. For example, if your friends are doing all the talking, then you are doing all the listening. This situation is not ideal because you are going to absorb too many emotions. Sometimes a quick topic change is necessary and encourages your friend to discuss other things with you. You might be listening to your friend droning on about their sibling's latest undesirable partner. Quite frankly, this situation is out of your control and has very little to do with you. When your friend takes a break, then simply change the topic to something you can talk about. Start with something like, "Before I forget, I wanted to tell you about the new yoga class I am attending. It allows you to talk and your friend can listen.

Remember that friends can help you cope with your emotions in other ways. At the same time, you can support them. What are some of the activities that you both like to do? Both of you might be into running, so schedule a weekly jog. You do not need to talk while out for a run but you still spend quality time together. Maybe you can even set a goal together, like training for an upcoming fun run in aid of charity. Or, your friends might admire your artistic side but are not very creative themselves. You could host a paint night with your friends and show them some painting techniques. These situations give an opportunity to build your own emotional strength while empowering your friends. It is an event that ticks all your empath boxes at once.

Best Friends

Empaths want friendships for life. Having occasional friends is not high on an empath's agenda because it is not fulfilling. Empaths appreciate friendships where both parties contribute equally and they will see these friendships as more important. Acquaintances often want to become great friends with empaths because of this long-lasting commitment. But, not all people do well around empaths.

Empaths usually select a few people to become close friends. Even if an empath is surrounded by people, they will only find one or two people that truly understand them. These best friends should support you and protect your emotions. They know that you give good advice, will listen to them, and understand their mood better than anyone else. But, these friends do not manipulate you or use you as an emotional punching bag. It is much better to have one very close friend than to have a big circle that simply exhausts you on every occasion.

Empaths have many qualities that make them desirable friends. They are active listeners but do not need their friends to speak about their emotions. Empaths immediately know the emotions of others and quickly adapt their attitude to support their friends in the best way possible. They do not even need to ask questions about a person. Your best friend will still know when they are starting to push you too far. A best friend gives an empath enough space to breathe and accepts that having alone time does not mean you are angry at them.

Having an empath as a best friend is like having a human lie detector. Your best friend will always listen to your opinion because they know your intuition is spot on. A new boyfriend will disappear from the scene quickly if you tell your friend that he is lying. Empaths pick up on dishonesty at the drop of a hat. So your best friend knows that you only have their interests at heart. An empath will often identify narcissists and energy vampires. They cannot stand fake friends and egotistical behavior. Empaths will alert friends about any person that acts in this way and eliminate them from the friendship circle.

Empaths are fun friends! They love nature, enjoy adventures, and thrive when doing new activities. You are probably going to be the person that invites your friends on a hike and picnic, or you might suggest something like rock climbing. Nature soothes your soul and gives you a chance to recharge emotionally. It also tests your physical strength and boosts your self-confidence when you achieve a new skill. Just remember that your friends might not be into all of these activities. Some of them may prefer reading or watching a movie. Try to balance your needs with those of your friends. If your best friend is not up for river rafting, then maybe just suggest a barbecue at the lake. Finding that balance makes it easier for both of you.

Your thrill-seeking nature makes you a perfect friend for traveling. Empaths are ambitious and do not say no to exploring new places. It allows empaths to get more world knowledge and satisfies emotional needs. Your best friend knows that traveling with you is an experience that they will not forget, so you are the first person they call to join them on their travels. Keep in mind that you still need some time alone. Do not share accommodation and keep to your normal routines as best possible. Enjoy the time with your friends and recharge your soul!

Chapter 6:
An Empath in Love

Every person wants a partner that loves them unconditionally. Empaths are some of the best partners in the world but can be some of the worst because they are so highly sensitive. Empaths love intensely. They put all their effort into making relationships successful. Some empaths seek the company of another empath; other empaths go for someone who is their total opposite.

Empaths love unconditionally. They are selfless individuals and most people have not felt love like this before. So your intense love might be a bit overwhelming at first. Yet, an empath's honesty makes their love sincere and fulfilling. Finding the right partner can take time and you might have your heart broken a few times. Empaths love deeply from the first day of the relationship, which can be overwhelming for your partner. But, meeting the right person is pretty incredible and you will know when it happens. Your empath intuition will alert you to the romantic spark and push you towards that person every day.

Empaths are averse to conflict and violence so they often watch comedies or drama. As an empath, you feel every romance deeply, even if it is a fictitious on-screen story. You pick up on the spark the moment that the main characters' eyes meet and you get a warm glowing feeling when the romance blossoms. You hurt deeply when one partner disrespects the other and you cannot stand the lying and cheating that appears so frequently in these movies. As one person runs away from the other, you feel their anguish and intense need to be alone. But, your heart rejoices when the story ends happily. A storybook romance is quite similar to what an empath experiences, even if other people think it is over-exaggerated emotions.

An Intense Love

An empath's relationship is different from others. Empaths seek uplifting romantic relationships that satisfy their internal needs. At the same time, they do not want to feel the relationship is taking over their lives and still need their time alone. This type of "hot and cold" romance is unique to empaths and can be challenging in relationships, especially if your partner is not an empath.

Empaths give everything in their relationships. They place their partner's wellbeing over their own, which is something that your partner will love. Some people describe empaths as angels in a relationship because they are patient, giving, and have supernatural love. This intense love is something that people may not be used to, so you need to pace yourself in the relationship.

Broken hearts are an inherent part of empaths. Ask any empath, they have had their hearts broken more than once. It might be from a relationship break-up but it can also be something entirely different. Empaths feel so greatly that their love extends to many things—nature, animals, and humanity. An empath can be heartbroken from violence in a foreign country or from interacting with toxic strangers. This heartbreak is not the fault of your partner. It is simply how you feel. Unfortunately, your partner might struggle with this concept and sudden heartbreak. They could feel they are at fault, even if you tell them otherwise. So be considerate of your emotions and set your partner's mind at ease.

Love for an empath is not just about emotions— empaths also need intimacy. An empath enjoys physical touch. Making love is a physical and psychological exercise. Empaths want to feel sensual and are open to new experiences in the bedroom. Yet, sex is not just about physical love. An empath needs an emotional connection. Empaths avoid one-night stands for this very reason. They want physical touch to be special and it can boost their mental state. Sex satisfies physical needs but an empath experiences much greater soul satisfaction.

Communication in Your Relationship

Honesty is the basis of all communication for empaths. An empath is always honest and expects honesty from their partner. They refuse to accept lies, even small ones. Empaths get upset when partners hide information. Your partner should know that you can see a lie from a mile away and that you will not tolerate it. The best option is to tell your partner this at the beginning of your relationship. Even better, emphasize the importance of honesty when you just start being interested in someone. Open communication will become the strength of your relationship because there are no hidden feelings.

Sometimes your partner will struggle with your involvement. An empath may become so emotionally involved in the lives of their partner that it suffocates the other person. You may be nurturing, but do not become a parent to your partner. Empaths should not force their partners to talk about things they do not want to. Empaths need time to process their own emotions and your partner needs this time too. Your partner will open up to you when the time is right.

No Cheating Here

Empaths are not prone to cheating. They do not want to hurt their partners so they remain committed to one person for the entire relationship. Empaths are not easily tempted to engage with other potential partners because they are way too busy thinking about other things. They simply do not have the time or energy to focus on cheating. This honesty in the relationship comes through in their love for their partners. But sometimes, your partner may feel you are cheating because you are spending time on other things and not paying them enough attention. Your partner does not want to play second fiddle to other people's issues or your latest humanitarian project.

Use your emotional connection and honesty to communicate with your partner about your priorities in life. Explaining the important things makes it easier for your partner to accept your projects or lengthy times away from the relationship. Your partner wants to know what you are up to, but they do not always want to take part in the event. Tell your partner about upcoming events or causes that you are pursuing before you start on these events. It will create an atmosphere of trust with your partner. They will know you are not avoiding the relationship but simply channeling your energy into another priority. Communicating your intentions also helps your partner to support you in the best way possible.

Sharing Emotions

An empath's honesty makes it easy for them to communicate with their partners. Your partner will know how you feel about all kinds of things. They know when you are heartbroken or need time on your own. Sharing your emotions with your partner is very important if you want your relationship to work. Explain to your partner that you will need some time alone when the world becomes too much, but do not isolate yourself entirely. Your partner does want to help you and can be a source of energy when you have none.

Some empaths find it difficult to communicate their emotions to their partners. Telling your partner how you feel is not the problem. The real issue is that some partners want to help you solve these issues, which only makes the time you spend thinking about it more. That is not good for your emotional wellbeing. An empath's partner sometimes thinks that getting involved with the situation will help you, but that is not always the case. You can control your own emotions and do not need your partner to protect you. But, for other people, protecting you comes naturally because they do not want to see you get hurt.

Empaths communicate with other people even in the absence of talking. They feel the emotions of others, especially their partners. This gut feel can be challenging for your partner. They might feel that you are intruding into their personal space. Sometimes an empath's partner will stop talking about their own emotions because they do not want you to get upset. Your partner might want to protect you from their feelings. But, you can still feel it anyway. So be honest with your partner—you do not need emotional protection. You want to share good and bad times. Communicating with each other is much better. Just assure your partner that you will cope with the additional emotions in your way. Healing always comes from the inside.

Stay in The Moment

Relationships can be challenging for anyone, even more so for an empath. Focusing on relationships takes time and energy. These factors make it difficult for empaths to fully embrace the needs of a relationship. But, you can concentrate on your relationship and your spiritual well-being simultaneously. The most important thing to remember is to stay in the moment. Your moment might be giving attention to your partner but it could also be alone time to help you cope with your emotions. Staying in the moment means you are aware of your needs and your partner's needs. You value each other's love, time, and emotions. It means being grateful for what your partner brings to your life.

Coping When Everything Becomes too Much

Relationships are great but also have their stress points. Your partner might not understand why you are upset, one of you could be withdrawn, and sometimes partners just do not understand each other. Your relationship just feels like too much. Empaths also worry about a million other things. It might be world hunger, a natural disaster, or a friend that is struggling. Worrying about these things just adds more relationship stress, especially if your partner does not always understand your concern. Empaths need to cope with all these issues while maintaining a healthy relationship.

Many empaths stop caring for themselves when they are in a relationship. You might focus too much on your partner. Your hobbies, meditation, and mental wellbeing are all placed to the wayside. Stepping out of your mental wellness routine can decrease your happiness and emotional intelligence. Empaths need to pay attention to their mental health while still caring for their partners. So make sure you spend time on your own activities.

Empaths need time alone even when they are in a relationship. Be upfront about your time alone from the start of your relationship. Being on your own gives you time to work through your feelings and recharge yourself emotionally. Alone time could be going to an exercise class, spending time in your studio, or even just retreating to another room to read.

Compromise

All relationships require compromise from partners. There are always disagreements or little things that crop up in relationships. These things are not a big issue, they just irritate the heck out of a person. But your relationship is great in all other areas, so breaking up about small things is just silly. Yet, you still need to talk about these irritants and come to a compromise.

Compromising does not mean that one person gives in. It means that you come to an agreement that suits both of you. Unfortunately, the nature of an empath often allows them to be manipulated or give in to the demands of their partner. Your partner might not even have asked you to compromise your boundaries but you still do it anyway. If your needs are second to your partner by your own decision, then the boundaries are blurry. Sacrifice does not come from one side only; it is a mutual decision from both partners.

Solving problems on your own is not the answer. Empaths have the ability to argue with themselves in their head. They might even have preconceived ideas of what their partners will say about the issue. Stop creating situations in your mind! You cannot control what the other person is going to say. Even though your intuition is great, you are not a mind reader. The argument playing out in your mind might be entirely unnecessary and all you are doing is already coming to a compromise. Rather, spend time on breathing exercises and clearing your mind. Then, talk to your partner and listen to their responses objectively. Coming to a reasonable agreement is probably easier than you think.

Empaths must talk about one specific compromise from the beginning. Animals. This topic will come up very quickly. Empaths love animals and always have pets around. Not all people are open to the idea of pets so you need to talk about animals and what is acceptable. Luckily, talking about animals is something that will pop up when you get to know each other. It is probably a question you will ask simply to get to know a person better. If a potential partner refuses to have pets, then this person is probably not right for you. On the other hand, you could come to a compromise about animals in your relationship. You might want several pets at once but your partner only wants one. So a good compromise could be to have one pet at a time or have one attention-seeking pet (like a dog) and some tropical fish that do not require constant affection.

Give Romance a Chance

Too many empaths give up on relationships. They worry about getting hurt and do not want to hurt the other person. Stop fearing intimacy. You might get hurt in your attempts at finding love. Just get back up after working through your emotions and move on to a new potential partner. If you struggle with relationships then take things slowly. Go on a date one weekend but keep the next weekend open for yourself. There is no rush to meet someone's parents or friends. Be honest with the other person and set a later date for these goals. Once your partner understands your emotional needs better, they will also give you the time you need to plan for new things.

Empaths are reluctant to step outside their comfort zones. They avoid relationships without even giving them a chance. Start pushing the boundaries of your comfort zone–go on a date or even just try sending a message to your crush. Otherwise, you will regret missing out on these times later on. Try something new with your partner–be adventurous! Join a couple's dance class, pick date night activities from a jar, or start a DIY project together. It is a fun way to get to know your partner in a setting that neither of you is familiar with. You have a chance to grow closer together.

Romantic relationships are a challenge for empaths. It takes all your mental strength to overcome potential issues and to reconcile when things go badly. Relationships can be a big stressor, especially if your partner does not understand you. An abusive and demeaning partner quickly breaks down an empath, which decreases their mental and emotional strength very quickly. An abusive relationship will never work for you. But, if the issues are everyday disagreements, then fight for your relationship. Ask your partner to be patient as you embark on a journey of improving your mental strength. Just as with friendships, your romantic relationship should be a safe space for personal growth.

An empath in love creates the foundation for a special relationship. You will love wholeheartedly, make your relationship a priority, and enjoy your partner immensely. Balance this love with spending time on your own. You might want to change your normal routines slightly, but just keep out some time for self-care. Looking after yourself is crucial to being an available partner. Immerse yourself into the relationship fully and look after each other's needs.

Chapter 7:
Empaths at Work

Every person has to work. Your personality and capabilities are likely to influence your career choice. As an empath, you have special gifts that make you ideal to work in certain fields. Each person is unique and not all careers are suitable for every empath. Evaluate your life, abilities, skills, and what you enjoy to help you find the best career.

Best and Worst Careers

A successful career provides fulfillment and meaning to life. Some people follow in their parents' footsteps, others follow a specific dream. Regardless of how you choose your line of work, empaths need to ensure they select a field where they can flourish. One option is to consider the type of empath you are and select a profession in this way.

Emotional Empaths

As an emotional empath, you easily identify the feelings of those around you. Emotional empaths are excellent friends but can experience periods of sadness. Emotional empaths have to practice self-care. Fatigue occurs easily so look after your own emotions too, otherwise it will decrease the effectiveness of your work.

Emotional empaths should choose a career where they can help others. A role at a non-profit organization is ideal. You might consider working for a charity where you partake in administration, small group tutoring, or organizing an event. Many emotional empaths perform better in a remote role because it provides space from emotionally charged interactions.

There are some jobs that emotional empaths should avoid. Many people think that emotional empaths can work in the medical field or large groups. This is not the case. There are too many emotions running rampant in medical practices and hospitals. Emotional empaths struggle to cope with these situations. Rather, help people from afar and look after yourself too.

Physical Empaths

Physical empaths often feel the pain and exuberance of those around them. It is natural for you to consider a career where you can help to fix people's problems. You probably feel happiest when other people have physical wellness. Some physical empaths select a career in sports or nutrition. You might consider coaching a sport's team or creating diet plans for others. A less physical option is a job where you can make visible changes for individuals. So, you could work in the construction industry.

Physical empaths sometimes choose medical professions. They have the ability to help heal physical ailments. Unfortunately, you can only succeed in this career if your emotions remain under control. Additionally, physical empaths may struggle to work in jobs where many people are hurting–it overwhelms their senses. Physical empaths fare well in careers that positively enable other individuals.

Intuitive Empaths

Although all empaths have great intuition, some empaths experience exceedingly high levels of intuitive abilities. They understand things unsaid and unseen through their gut feeling. You might consider an abstract career, specifically in therapeutic fields. Intuitive empaths excel in social work and counseling because they get people to open up easily. Working with vulnerable individuals like the elderly, orphans, or the mentally ill is a good option. Some intuitive empaths select political or legal careers to create change in society. You are part of a small percentage of empaths that succeed in high-pressure careers.

Intuitive empaths require careers with impact. They are unsatisfied with mundane and repetitive jobs. Avoid general office work or production line activities. You probably will not do well in generic positions. A more abstract option is to express yourself through art, music, or graphic design.

Flora Empaths

Flora empaths enjoy nature, especially plants. You probably already cultivated a garden, grown your own veggies, and looked after the office plants. Plant empaths are natural caregivers so these types of roles are ideal. You will do well working in a nursery, both the plant type or a children's nursery. Plant empaths often enjoy activism, biochemical research, and gardening. A career in garden landscaping is a popular choice for many flora empaths.

Plant empaths do not have to work with plants or outdoors. Some flora empaths struggle with gardening-type careers as they do not want to trim plants or chop trees. It might hurt you to reign in plants, so it is better to stick to jobs that allow for growth. Focus your career dreams on environmental sciences, youth development, or join a company with 'green' priorities.

Earth Empaths

Mother earth is your top priority. You feel that every person should look after the earth and adopt environmentally-friendly practices. Most earth empaths opt for careers that foster a connection with the globe or become activists. Ecology, weather patterns, and ecosystems are things that interest you. Good career choices include education, environmental policy creation through activism, or protection of indigenous species. Some earth empaths enjoy careers in gardening or do town planning with an emphasis on green solutions. Alternative energy, like solar power and wind turbines, is something that may appeal to you.

Earth empaths can handle their emotions regarding the culling of dangerous plants. Your focus is on the preservation of natural resources, even if it means sacrificing other elements of nature. Your ability to see the bigger picture means you can take a leadership role, while smaller details may slip your mind. However, earth empaths can be unpopular among colleagues due to their staunch opposition to strategies, so make sure that you choose a job where you fit in and have values that align with your beliefs.

Animal Empaths

Animal lovers have several career options. You might bond strongly with animals so volunteering at an animal shelter or animal refuge center is an option. Being able to nurse animals back to health and reunite them with new families will motivate you. Nature conservation is another good option, or studying zoology can be useful. Animal care comes naturally to you, so any career where you empower animals works for you. Pet sitting, a grooming shop, or walking dogs are all good ideas.

Becoming a vet might seem like a good idea but most animal empaths cannot handle seeing hurt animals. They shudder at the thought of euthanizing animals or treatments that may harm an animal. So, veterinary care is not always the best option. Rather, focus on educating people about other options to euthanasia and saving animals in their natural habitats. Many animal empaths are vegan or vegetarian, so you might consider a career in health foods or activism.

Corporate Culture

Every company has specific ways of doing things. The values, beliefs, work ethic, and setup of an organization create the company culture. You have your own culture, or background, which makes you unique and has shaped aspects of your life. You might be a hard worker, believe that others should be placed first, and that environmental protection is the responsibility of all members of society. Similarly, a business might value optimal employee efficiency, believe the client is king, and contribute to society through charitable donations.

Corporate culture is immersive. Considering corporate culture is crucial when selecting a prospective employer. You do not want to end up in an organization that does not have the same ideals as you. Culture is the largest motivator for doing your best at work. Empaths have specific characteristics that make it even more important for them to find a good cultural fit. Every employer has their own rules and code of conduct, which might not be the same as your beliefs. An effective empath at work accepts these differences, within reason, and works to the best of their abilities.

The workplace is fast-paced, action-packed, and unpredictable. These things are not always the best for empaths as they need structure, peace, and the ability to think logically. Before entering a new job, you need to know what you are getting yourself into. Empaths need positions that align with their beliefs and method of operation. Any career requires working alongside other people. Empaths feel the emotions of others, so the workplace can become overwhelming, especially if there are a lot of people coming in and out.

Find a job that suits your personality. Visiting a company website gives lots of information about the organization and its beliefs. Oftentimes, you can see a list of the company's values and read about the working environment. Empaths get an intuitive feel of a company by speaking to former and current employees. It is a great way to determine if you will fit in at a new job. One specific thing you want to look at is corporate responsibility initiatives–these are activities that a company engages in to enrich society and the greater environment. Charity drives, volunteering, and donations are all things that may appeal to your inner goodwill.

Your Best Work

Empaths are excellent workers because of their intuition, attention to detail, and consideration of others. Your best work happens when you are in the right role and have the necessary organizational support. Empaths that are constantly unhappy in a position or feel smothered should wonder if they are in the right role. Select a company where colleagues value each other, have mutual respect, and share similar values. Empaths do well in companies with less than 20 employees and work in small teams. They become effective and efficient in roles with integrity and take responsibility for the outcomes from their work.

Empaths often flourish in leadership roles at work. It allows empaths to feel proud of other people. Not all empaths want a leadership role with lots of responsibility as it causes too much stress. You might just want to lead a club at work or take on a mentoring role with new employees. Empath leadership empowers job performance positively. Your motivation is infectious and could make the whole team more productive. Empaths can lead training well because they know when people are stuck or struggle to understand the topic. Leadership by empaths comes from active listening and concentrating on team effectiveness.

Balance is necessary for your best work to take place. Your perception is already great, but be careful of becoming overly sensitive to the emotions of colleagues, especially when it has nothing to do with work. Empaths that isolate their emotions from work do better in fulfilling multiple roles. Positivity and gratitude towards colleagues serve the greater purpose of the company. An empath's strategic thinking skills helps to focus on organizational goals and enables planning to achieve a shared vision.

Stay Objective

Emotions are subjective. Our bodies elicit an emotional response to events and empaths have an even greater reaction. This reaction can be an issue at work. You cannot allow your emotions to control your life at work. Ignoring or suppressing your emotions is not something that comes to you naturally, so you need to make a conscious effort. The corporate world is not the same as you are, so empaths have to use their communication skills and mental strength in overcoming their emotions.

Empaths can consider several viewpoints. Sometimes, these viewpoints do not agree with our beliefs and it upsets us. You are likely to realize organizational issues, changes, or HR decisions before these are communicated by management. Working with colleagues also makes you realize that not everyone's the same. Yet, you must remain objective.

Acknowledging the shortcomings of corporate culture is important for empaths. Not only are there cultural issues, but people also portray different behaviors. Accept that some people are not kind. You cannot expect every colleague to be friendly, positive, or kind. You are not at work to fix your colleagues or their problems. In fact, some colleagues may push away your attempts at helping. It is not your responsibility to sort out problems outside of your work scope. Remain focused on your role and protect your emotions, so that you can be objective in all organizational interactions.

Coping at Work

There are days when work is great and other days when you question whether it is worth your time. Stress, negativity, and inappropriate behavior are all part of the working world. An empath attunes their senses to the feelings of colleagues, which can ruin a good day very quickly. You might realize a work friend is upset about not getting a promotion, or feel the exuberant joy when a peer hits a new sales target. Regardless of the type of emotion, empaths have to protect themselves and focus on their work. Absorbing the stress of colleagues counteracts your talents and diminishes your work ethic. Empaths require emotional resilience in the work environment to be assertive and avoid bullying or manipulation.

A Protective Bubble

Have you seen those large inflatable balls that people can get into? It is like a huge protective bubble that pads you from falling and getting hurt. They almost look like the balls that hamsters run around in but are just a suitable size for humans. These inflatable bubbles are a great metaphor for your mental health at work. Place yourself in an imaginary bubble before you start your workday. It will help to protect your feelings. Anytime that a colleague attempts to push their emotions onto you, simply push it out of the way with your mental bubble. Nothing can penetrate your emotional shield. Just roll right over the issue and continue with your work.

There are times when your ball might break or get some cracks in it. You need to protect yourself against these times and quickly patch the bubble. One way to protect yourself at work is to limit the interactions that you have with negative colleagues. Unfortunately, you cannot ignore colleagues or avoid them entirely because they are part of the company too. But, you can approach these individuals with care and responsible communication.

Engaging with toxic colleagues requires protective strategies. You do not want to make yourself prey to negative emotions or attitudes. Every workplace has gossip at the watercooler or a person that constantly badmouths other employees. Empaths often listen to these things because manipulators know they will get a reaction from them. It is best to avoid these situations entirely. Do not engage in office gossip. One way to stop a colleague quickly is to simply say, "I have to go finish a report," or, "My next meeting starts in a few minutes, so I have to go now." Most people will then seize their talking. If it is a particularly difficult person, then excuse yourself and immediately walk away.

A Productive Workspace

Productivity and efficiency happen when a person has a dedicated workspace. Empaths need structure to do their best, so your workspace is very important for your mental health. Open-plan offices are not suitable for empaths because there are too many emotions floating around. It is best to have a separate desk in an office or at least a dedicated workstation shared with other team members. Keep your workspace tidy and check that all your things are ready for work before leaving for home. It sets the scene for a conducive working environment.

Many empaths prefer remote working or have their own business. This solitude empowers them to work better and shield them from emotions. They do not have to deal with office politics. Even if you have a fulltime job, your boss might allow you to work from home a few days a week. A home office is always a good idea but make sure that other things do not distract you in your office. Keep a strict work schedule, note all your appointments and deadlines, and ensure you take frequent breaks during the day.

Being Your Own Boss

A strong-willed and confident empath can run their own business quite easily. Even if you lack self-confidence, working for yourself remains an option. Many empaths find that working for themselves provides the level of responsibility that they seek and can improve their mental strength. However, manage your stress properly and never take on more than you are comfortable with as it affects your resilience.

Empaths have many opportunities for building their own business. A plant empath may run their own gardening business or grow vegetables to sell at local markets. An animal empath could do well with a home-grooming service or set up a parlor. One-on-one personal training is an option for physical empaths. Intuitive and emotional empaths might do freelance writing from the comfort of their home. The options are endless so focus on your abilities to decide on your business.

Just because you are your own boss does not mean you cannot do without help. Knowledgeable assistance is essential for empaths as it splits the workload. Each person has their own strengths and you know your weaknesses. If numbers are a weak point, then get an accountant to do your bookkeeping. If you struggle with admin, then employ a part-time or full-time assistant. You are not in this boat alone. Find people and resources that complement your strengths and soon you will have a sustainable business.

Chapter 8:
The Roller Coaster

Life is a roller coaster. There are ups and downs, twists and turns, one moment you are on top of the world and the next you accelerate into water. Empaths experience life as an abundant roller coaster of events and emotions.

Helping others and making a difference keeps you moving uphill. The birth of a sibling or a friend that gets married is a positive thing for you. Having an impact on your colleagues and environment can keep the momentum going, even if it is a slow pace moving towards a peak. Maybe your life seems to be going very well–you have a partner who cares, your friends understand your empathic needs, and daily life is fulfilling. You are positive and smiling all the way. Then suddenly, it all comes crashing down.

Something tips life over the edge. The roller coaster cart seems to lose its balance and all you see is the ground approaching at breakneck speed. A loved one passes on, a family member is diagnosed with a serious illness, or you lose your job. The bad events may not even be as direct because empaths are alert to everything. Global unrest, terror attacks in other countries, and activism all affect an empath. It is part of the scenery on your roller coaster ride. Some backdrops last longer than others or time passes slowly. The ride becomes prolonged and you just want to get off.

Each person has their own roller coaster. In the theme park of life, you can see other people's rides. Their lows might intersect with your roller coaster and their high points put a smile on your face. These feelings are normal because of your intuitive abilities and attachment to other people. The anticipation for the next part of the ride is palpable. Your heart races and you have to take off. You need to look to the future if you want to move forward, even if it is a difficult time in your life.

Theme parks and roller coasters are exciting and frightening at the same time. Sometimes, we stand in awe looking up at a monster and wonder if the ride will be exhilarating or downright awful. Empaths want to feel the adrenaline rush. They thrive on the highs of life and dread the lows. But many times we judge a ride before getting on it. It is too high, too fast, or has too many twists and turns. Stop doing that. Stop judging the ride and keep your feet on the ground. Focus on the experience because you cannot predict what life will throw at you, even if you do see it approaching.

The Highs and Lows

Take a moment to think about your life. Grab a piece of paper and draw your rollercoaster. It does not have to be pretty, just a simple line will do. What happened in the last few months or year? Are you moving up on your rollercoaster, or do you feel a devastating downturn?

Now think about the future. Do you know of some events that will improve your rollercoaster? Maybe you are pregnant and the imminent birth of your child is something positive happening in the next few months. Or the charity you work for is close to reaching their fundraising goal. Draw those lines into your rollercoaster. You might know that something negative is going to happen and it is okay to add those to your rollercoaster. You need to draw those lines. What you cannot draw are things you do not know will happen. You cannot put in "something bad"–remain positive.

Roller coasters have many lessons to teach us. Sometimes a person looks at a roller coaster and thinks "there is no way I am going on that ride." That is perfectly fine. Not every person's life has to be part of yours and you do not have to be a feature in theirs. You will never please everyone, so move on to the rides that make your soul happy. Some people's rides are so broken, that approaching them is going to take way too much of your time and hurt you in the long run. At times, the wheels of your cart seem like they are going to come off but you should not back down. Rather, find the problem in your roller coaster and fix it. Invest time and energy into improving yourself and your ride becomes more attractive to others.

The great thing is that you can make a difference in good and bad times. You can control your roller coaster or at least your responses to sudden track changes. It is possible to affect the rollercoaster that others are on as well.

Assisting during Tumultuous Times

Empaths have a desire to help. They want to affect change, be available to their friends and family, and make things better. But, the overwhelming events and emotions from the lives of others can cause you to feel negative. It can derail your roller coaster cart. So, you need strategies to cope in life and assist people in the best way possible. These are skills that keep you focused, help in calming your mind, and give an opportunity to make a difference.

Never over-commit to someone else's problems. Just because you are willing to help does not mean you should do everything or be taken advantage of by a person going through difficulty. Control your time carefully and tell your friend when you need to go. They will understand, you do not need to feel bad about leaving. Your friend or family member knows that you care and showing up just proves this point. Protect the boundaries you have set for yourself. The boundaries in good times should still apply during challenges.

Empaths can just be there. Simply having the company already steadies many people. One person may want to talk about the bad event and empaths great listening skills are ideal. Remember that the person might have had a traumatic experience but can still focus on good things as well. If your best friend just lost their sibling to a tragic accident, then they may be overcome with sadness. Help the person by remembering good times, like sharing a fond memory or a joke that the deceased always told. Sometimes all the person needs is to have companionship without talking at all–they just do not want to be alone. So take a book to read or maybe pack your art supplies to keep you busy productively at your friend's place.

Practical assistance is something that can bring joy to you and help the suffering person. People forget about everyday tasks when they struggle or they just do not have the energy to complete mundane activities. These actions make the situation worse, so you might offer your help in other ways than just emotionally. Offer to take care of their pets, maybe even take them home with you if necessary. Animals soothe the souls of empaths, so it is a win-win situation. You could clean the house, water the plants, or pick their clothes up from the laundry. Cooking a meal is great therapy for you and provides nourishment for the other person. You do not need to do everything yourself–you can always place an order somewhere and get products delivered to your friend's house. Sometimes physical support improves the emotional state of the other person.

Finding the positive in a bad situation brings hope. Empaths are a beacon of support and hope for people going through tough times. Your role is one of motivation and support. It might not be easy to see the light at the end of the tunnel but it is there. Empaths are easily overcome by the emotions of struggling friends or family, so you need to keep up your own energy by focusing on the glimmer of light in every dark situation. For example, if a peer loses their job but has a passion for rebuilding bicycles, then you might motivate them to turn their hobby into a money-making opportunity. Or when a friend has to move to a new town you can remind them that it is a chance to make additional friends. Always look for the silver lining.

Do not forget about yourself in the process of helping. Sometimes empaths get so wrapped up in the lives of others that they let their own emotional and physical health slide. Do not let it happen because it will make you less effective in helping. Take time out after being with your upset friend to deal with your own emotions. Write your feelings down in a journal or meditate to recharge your soul. Allow all the emotions to flow over you. Engage in a productive activity after emotional encounters like volunteering at a shelter, doing something creative, or going for a jog.

You Cannot Control Everything

Repeat it to yourself: I cannot control everything. Take time to think about what you have just said. You cannot control the universe. You can only feel its pain and joy. Some things are entirely out of your control and you need to accept this fact. Natural disasters happen–you cannot stop the trembling of an earthquake or the destruction of a tsunami. There is absolutely no way that you should feel emotionally responsible for these events. Life happens in unexpected ways.

Be mindful of your own thoughts during tumultuous times. Stop trying to solve all the problems. It will only bring you down in the long run. Reconnect with yourself and identify the issues that you need to let go of. Ignore the critical voice inside of your mind because it only spreads negativity, especially when you are already feeling down. Even though your curiosity wants satisfaction, there is no way that you will ever have all the answers to life's issues. Life events are complicated and sometimes trying to sort out a problem crosses the boundaries you have set up.

Anchor your thoughts on what you can control. Empaths can get lost in emotions so you need coping strategies. It is best to be an observer of events rather than immersing yourself in situations beyond your control. Think about it as a movie and view it from the outside. You would not jump into the middle of an actual tsunami because you cannot swim through it, so do not throw yourself into emotional superstorms. Be the anchor to the boat and protect your emotions. Only then can you remain strong for the people around you. There are times when you need to leave the problems to the professionals, even if it means pushing a friend or family member to seek professional help. Suggesting something different may be exactly the help your friend needs to get back on track.

Put on Your Safety Belt

All theme parks have strict safety measures to protect their visitors. Your life is the theme park and your emotions are the visitors, so you need to create safety protocols. Put a safety belt on the roller coaster that is your life. This safety belt is your self-care. You have to put on your own safety equipment before you can help someone else with their equipment. Unfortunately, empaths often do it in the opposite order and forget about their own emotional safety. Take care of yourself first so that your emotional strength does not fall off the ride.

Remain Positive

An optimistic mindset is the first thing that empaths need to cope during bad times. You know the things that make you happy. Keep up with your normal daily routine so that you can recharge from difficult events. Drink lots of water for a physical detox of bad products, exercise often, and eat healthy meals. Empaths sometimes skip meals because they want to get to other things faster but this is a bad habit. If you are running around, then at least get a smoothie or juice to keep you going.

Sometimes the negative emotions become too much. These times are when you need to regroup and find your positivity. One way is to think about all the emotional baggage you are carrying. Imagine the space it takes up inside of your body. Now get out the vacuum cleaner and start to extract all those negative emotions. Feel yourself becoming weightless and see the clean, white light appearing and the vacuum cleaner sucks up your emotions. Focus on the clean surface that remains and appreciate the good times.

Surround yourself with positivity. Accept your role in events and be at peace with what is beyond your control. There is no room for negativity. Listen to upbeat music that represents how you want to feel. Sing along with the lyrics and dance about to get your endorphins pumping. Socialize with a friend that motivates you to feel good about yourself or spend time with your pets. Another option is to write down things you are thankful for or send an uplifting message to someone who needs encouragement.

Take a Break

Time alone is crucial for empaths that help other people. Be compassionate to yourself and practice self-love. Try to be as gentle with your own emotions as you are with the feelings of the people around you. Do not give in to erratic emotions but rather practice emotional resilience and manage your feelings carefully.

Spending time on your own is the best way to recharge your emotional batteries. It is general maintenance for the emotional roller coaster of life. Some empaths escape to a comforting nature spot or play an instrument. Other options are exercising or meditating. Ensure that you remove yourself entirely from the troublesome situation when you are alone. Switch off any electronic devices, do not reply to messages or emails, and avoid watching television if possible. This break should be for you alone and there is no space for media sources to interfere with your emotions.

Sometimes, tumultuous times make it challenging to find time alone. Yet, it is so important that you prioritize your own mental health. If you are pressed for time, then you might consider bringing together some of your routines. For example, you can practice self-care and meditation at the same time. Meditate while you shower. Turn the water to a warm temperature and let it run over your body. Imagine the dirt on your body as emotional dirt. Wash away the negativity. Acknowledge the emotions then lather them up with soap and scrub away. Close your eyes and just become aware of the situation. Look down as you rinse the soap from your body and see it swirling down the rain. Those soap suds are negative emotions that you have washed from your body. Take a few deep breaths and enjoy the feeling of refreshment and optimism.

Release Emotions

Emotions build up over time and become visitors in our bodies. They can create physical tension and stress, so it is very important to release your emotions frequently. Most empaths schedule time in their day to refocus. There are many ways to invigorate your soul but all of them have similar characteristics—identification, analysis, and acceptance.

Find a quiet place. You want an area where you can be alone and other people or things cannot disturb you. It might be a spot in the garden, a room in your house, or even the bathroom at a shopping center. Close your eyes and identify the area in your body that holds emotion. Maybe it is your shoulders because you are feeling the weight of the world, or over your abdomen from the butterflies flying about. Pay attention to that area and try to relax your muscles. You could even do it physically by massaging the spot or applying a soothing heat pack.

Focus on the tense area and give it a mental hug. Take a few deep breaths and exhale the emotions. It is a soothing exercise to tell yourself everything is okay. You might not be able to remove all the tension but that does not matter. Some discomfort is okay but do not let it consume you. Encourage yourself, focus on your positive traits, and know you are making a difference. Remain in the moment and remember that this experience is only a small part of the roller coaster ride of life.

Chapter 9:
Soothe Your Body, Mind, & Soul

Empaths need to look after themselves because of their sensitive nature. Throughout this book, we have explored several strategies to manage stress and cope. There are numerous strategies for you to live a better life, so explore all your options. Once you get your emotions under control, you can think clearly and make a difference. Empaths have so much to offer the world that their skills should be highlighted and not hidden. Empower yourself to live a better life and enact change.

Heal Yourself First

Empaths are aware of their emotions, even if their emotional intelligence is not well developed. You know when you feel happy, sad, and stressed. Becoming aware of your emotions is a mindfulness practice. Being mindful is simply being aware of your surroundings and staying in the moment. When you experience overwhelming emotions, take a moment to relax.

Relaxation is an essential need for empaths. It is an opportunity to recharge emotionally and physically. Empaths often neglect relaxation because they are too busy solving other people's problems. But, most empaths do spend time on their own and schedule it into their daily routine. This time alone is a period for relaxation, even if it is filled with tension. Taking a step away from the hustle and bustle of life will have a positive impact on you.

Relaxing is a beneficial activity for your mind, body, and soul When you relax, you breathe properly and oxygen circulates through your body. This enhanced circulation makes you more alert, decreases your blood pressure, and stabilizes your heart rate. In turn, you feel better and more energetic. Your skin and body will thank you because you are less tired. Relaxation can even reduce the effects of aging. Relaxing before bedtime improves your sleep and decreases restlessness. Relaxation quiets the mind and restores the body.

Grounding Exercises

Grounding is a relaxation technique that focuses on mindfulness. You experience the moment through your senses, which reconnects you to the earth and gives balance. It is common practice to do grounding exercises when you feel overwhelmed or anxious. You may be familiar with several of these grounding exercises already, but do you use them? Knowing about them is not enough. Choose at least one technique to incorporate into your day. Select one that you can do no matter where you are, even if it is a room full of people. Practice this one technique often, then introduce other techniques when you are ready. Soon, you will find a default grounding method that becomes a part of you, just like the air you breathe.

Physical Grounding

Physical methods require tangible objects or your senses. The idea is to focus on what you see, hear, smell, feel, and taste. By paying attention to your senses, your mind calms down and soothes your soul.

Heat and cold are often used in physical grounding. Think about how you feel when you soak in a warm bubble bath or jump into an icy lake. Your skin tingles and awakens your soul. For quick grounding, hold ice or a cold pack in your hands, then switch to a warm bean bag. Alternate between hot and cold and note how each switch makes you feel.

Food experiences provide grounding too. Do not just gulp down your food without a thought. Take a moment to feel the textures, see the colors, and focus on the taste. Is it sweet, salty, or sour? Do the same when you have a beverage. Feel the bubbles on your tongue from a soda, and the creaminess of a milkshake. Smell the cup of tea in your hand and the onions cooking on the stove.

A popular grounding technique is the 5-4-3-2-1. It is very useful in high-pressure situations and requires a great deal of attention. You constantly have to focus on the next step and become alert in the process. It allows you to forget about everything else for a moment and uses all your senses. There is one number for each sense but they do not have to be in a specific order. Just find things in your surroundings that you can see, touch, hear, taste, and smell. For example, from my desk, I can see five things: a pot plant, a computer, hand lotion, a glass, and a tree outside. I can touch four things: the keyboard, my shirt, paper, and a table lamp. I can hear three things: birds chirping outside, music playing, and a dog barking. I can taste two things: water and chewing gum. Finally, I can smell one thing, which is the room refreshing spray. Take a moment and try this technique yourself.

Mental Grounding

Mental grounding focuses the mind and relieves current stressful thoughts. Some mental methods can be done on your own, or you can involve a friend or romantic partner. Choose something that works for you and do not force a method that seems like a waste of time.

Recite a song, poem, or quote. Think about it quietly and visualize the words in your mind. Say the piece aloud while listening intently. Do not rush through it. Start over if you get stuck. Some people recite prayers in the morning or before bed to help them relax.

Play a word or numbers game. Crosswords, word searches, and sudoku are just a few of the available options. Make some time to play these games. There are many apps that you can download to play, or forget about the technology and go old school with pen and paper. Alternatively, choose a letter of the alphabet and write down as many words starting with that letter that you can think of. Another option is to recite times tables or count backwards from 50.

Use category thinking to create focus. Think about the charades game. A person selects a movie and then has to mime the title for others to guess. This is a typical mental grounding technique. You have to determine the genre, number of words in the title, and then figure out the name. Charades is a team game but you can play category games alone. Think about all the frozen yogurt flavors you have tasted or list all the football teams you know.

There are many activities and games that provide mental grounding. Build a puzzle, find the difference between two pictures, or play memory games. Another option is to write down instructions for your favorite recipe or explain a task to yourself. Most mental activities provide grounding but we do them without a thought. Pay attention while doing these tasks and congratulate yourself afterwards.

Soothing Methods

Soothing your mind is another way to ground yourself. It provides an opportunity to reminisce, experience love, and be compassionate. These methods work exceptionally well when your emotions are getting the better of you. Try one of the techniques below to uplift yourself or just as a reminder that you are worthy of love and a great person. Soothing methods are a great follow up for mental and physical grounding, as you are focused enough to appreciate yourself.

Be kind to yourself. Compassion is a skill that empaths have for others but seldom apply it to themselves. What is your biggest problem right now? Change this problem by motivating yourself. For example, say to yourself, "It is difficult but I am doing my best." Repeat this mantra over and over again. Write it down and place it within your view. Stick it onto your computer screen, wall, or mirror. The more you read it, the more you believe it.

Think of a living thing you love. It can be the face of a loved one, your pet, or even a plant. Picture them in your mind. See their face, eyes, and smile. Can you hear their voice? Think about the experiences you shared with this love and what about them makes you happy. Spend a moment telling them your issue (in your mind) and imagine what their response would be. They are probably very proud of the empath you are and value you in their life.

Spend time in comfort. All of us have something that brings us peace, so do what makes your heart happy. For some people, it is a blanket from childhood. Others might feel peace when they feel water running over their skin. Maybe you find comfort when you wear a specific t-shirt. Listen to your favorite song or watch a feel-good movie. These activities make you feel like yourself and give you a mental boost.

Your favorite things might just be the key to happiness. Grab a piece of paper and pen and write down some of your favorite things. Anything goes: food, places, people, animals, plants, activities. Why are these your favorite things? This is a type of gratitude exercise so take your time thinking about these things. To motivate you some more, indicate when you will be in contact with your favorite things. You might only have an hour left before you see your beloved cat, or your mom is visiting over the weekend. Use these events to keep you positive. If it is still some time before you can do these things, then start planning your next encounter. Maybe you can look at dates for your next holiday or schedule a dinner date with your friends.

Meditate

Meditation is a hot topic for relaxation. It is a spiritual practice but you do not have to be religious to meditate. Most empaths already feel a connection to the world in a spiritual sense, which makes meditation a good relaxation and soothing technique. There are many different forms of meditation, so find one that works for you. Try to meditate at least once a day. If you are going through a difficult time, then meditate twice or even three times a day. Meditation takes anywhere from a few minutes up to an hour or longer, depending on your choice.

Motionless Meditation

Meditation and discipline are two sides of the same coin. They require determination and commitment to a clean mind. Many meditative practices require you to sit or stand still while breathing deeply. There are many meditative positions. There is no right or wrong position, so focus on what works best for you. Practice discipline by remaining in this position for several minutes. You can keep your hands next to your sides or press the palms of your hands together. But, there are many other hand and leg positions too.

Start by getting into a comfortable position in a quiet area. You can kneel in the garden, sit with crossed legs on the floor, or even lie on a flat surface. Make sure you are comfortable. Take a few deep breaths and release the tension in your body. Close your eyes. Place your hands in a prayer position with the palms and fingertips touching. Breathe in deeply for a few counts and then release your breath. Clear your mind of all thoughts and focus on being aware of your breathing. If your thoughts start to dwell, then press the fingertips of your middle finger together lightly and focus only on them. It should help you refocus. Continue breathing deeply until you are calm.

Meditating in Busy Places

Empaths become overwhelmed in busy situations. There are so many emotions floating around the room that you want to get away. Unfortunately, it is not always possible to remove yourself from the area. You can meditate right there where you are, whether it be at your desk or in a bustling conference room.

Sit up straight and comfortable in your seat. Relax your shoulders, neck, and back. Place your feet on the floor and your hands in front of you. Take a few deep breaths to circulate oxygen through your body. Next, look around you and observe the objects in the room. Name them as you see them but do not pass judgment or allow yourself to get irritated. Simply name them in your mind… desk, chair, window, books… Continue to breathe deeply as you quiet your emotions.

Meditate with Movement

Some people cannot sit still. They struggle with meditation because they want to move around. Animal and plant empaths frequently struggle with this issue because they want to do things. Luckily, you can meditate even while moving. Yoga is the quintessential moving meditation technique. It focuses on breathing while moving your body through a series of stretches. You still have to hold each stretch for several seconds, so there are elements of discipline. But, you can exercise and meditate at the same time. Find a yoga class near you to learn the breathing technique and start moving.

Enlightenment

Enlightenment is linked to insight. Enlightening meditation is a great option for intuitive empaths. You might even have visionary or intuitive thoughts during the meditation process. This meditative technique focuses on breathing and deeper consciousness.

Always find a quiet and safe space to meditate. Make sure it is free of distractions so that you can focus on meditation. Breathe deeply and hold the breath for a few counts before releasing it. Exhale negative energy and inhale positivity. As the new breath moves through your body, become aware of how it moves into your lungs and the expansion of your chest. Once your mind is calm, start thinking about a mantra that provides positivity for a specific situation. Some people add props, such as a person's photo, to help focus their intention.

Forgiveness

Meditation helps with overcoming emotions. Anger or resentment are issues that empaths struggle with often and may pop up during meditation. You can use your meditation time for practicing forgiveness. Use it to forgive yourself or other people.

Use the basic meditative technique of sitting still for your meditation. Take deep breaths that expand your lungs, so that oxygen circulates through your bloodstream. Start by thinking of a mantra for this situation. For example, "I release my fear of failure." While inhaling, consider the event that you should forgive yourself for. Repeat your mantra while you exhale and release any negativity energy. Do this several times. If you need to forgive a specific person, you can meditate on the event and a mantra that forgives the person. Shift your thoughts between the person and mantra until you find peace.

Energy

The body contains seven energy centers, called chakras. These centers run from the bottom of your spine to the crown of your head. All seven chakras are in a straight line, which provides alignment. Each chakra corresponds to a part of the endocrine system. The endocrine glands release hormones that cause and relieve stress. When each of your chakras is open, you have good energy emanating from your body and it releases positive hormones. But, when your chakras are closed or overactive, you experience negativity and oversensitivity from negative hormone release.

With energy meditation, the focus is on opening and balancing each energy center. Start by lying on your back in a comfortable position. Close your eyes and breathe deeply. Clear all thoughts from your mind. Next, you have to focus on each chakra for several breaths until the tension in that area releases.

Energy meditation always starts at the lowest chakra and moves up the spine. Focus on the root chakra at the bottom of your spine, which is responsible for emotions such as trust. Next, move to the sacral chakra located between your hips for increased sexual and creative energy. The area above the belly button, or solar plexus chakra, is responsible for feelings of power and greater wisdom. Focus your attention in the middle of your chest for the heart chakra that governs healing and love. The next chakra is in the throat and provides communicative energy, which is essential for empaths. The third eye chakra is between the eyes and helps with awareness. At the crown of the head is the chakra responsible for spirituality, so it is useful for intuitive and emotional empaths. Once you have focused energy on each chakra, continue taking a few deep breaths. Slowly open your eyes and feel the extra energy pulsing through your body.

Empaths have so many thoughts running through their minds and want to do a million different things in one day. Realize that you are just one person and cannot get to everything. You need time alone to rest and recharge. Ask yourself whether these activities are beneficial to you and will the world end if you do not help immediately. Take time for yourself every day. Stop and breathe. Close your eyes and become conscious of the air around you. Feel the wind blowing against your skin and the glow from the sun. Spend time doing the things you love, be grateful, and live an inspired life.

Chapter 10:
Thrive as an Empath

Empaths can live a positive and impactful life! It is not easy to be an empath, especially because we feel everything so deeply. Negative energy easily creeps upon us and we feel the pain of the world. But, you do not have to accept this negativity. You can live your best life! All you need to do is harness your special empath gifts and maintain focus on the end goal: to leave a lasting, positive impression on the world.

Acknowledge Your Talents

Every person has talents. These talents are gifts that make us unique and give purpose to our lives. Some people are good at playing sports or have a keen sense of mathematics. You probably already know what your talents are, but did you know that empaths have additional talents? All empaths share five special gifts. These gifts are something you may be aware of, or you might not realize that you have these additional strengths. Awareness of these talents allows you to harness their power and have a bigger impact. They empower you to do your best and improve your self-love.

How do I know what my talents are? This question crosses the minds of empaths frequently.

Overwhelming emotions and a lack of self-confidence may hide your true talents. You need to focus on improving your life and managing your emotions if you want to use your talents properly. Luckily, identifying your talents is a confidence booster and can bring balance to your life. Start by considering what you do well and your competencies. These skills may shed light on your talents. Alternatively, ask your friends and family what they think your talents are. Think back to your memories and times you excelled to help in discovering your gifts.

Talents are beneficial to you, your friends and family, and the greater community. Other people experience your gifts and find them motivating. By using your talents productively, others see you as a role model and follow your example. Children and adolescents look to older individuals for inspiration. Be a positive influence in their lives. So, talents are mutually beneficial for you and those interacting with you.

The ability to live out your talents has health benefits. Making a difference improves your health because it decreases your stress levels and gives a sense of purpose. You do not feel as much pressure to perform since you use your talents confidently. Having special gifts boosts positivity and adds vitality to your life. It decreases your anger and sadness, so you might even experience less physical pain. You focus on doing your best because you enjoy what you are doing. This optimism is contagious and others appreciate your effort.

Empaths are not normal. They are superhuman beings with the ability to conquer whatever life throws at them. You can make a huge difference in the lives of those around you, greater society, and the world as a whole. But, it can only happen if you decide to use your talents for good. It means you have to be proactive, listen to yourself, and appreciate that your gifts are not understood by everybody. Now is the time to start using your empath talents. Do not put it off any longer. You know which talents you already use well, so focus on keeping them going. Then, start working on your other gifts and improve yourself little by little. A first step can go a long way. So, what are the empath gifts?

Vision

Empaths have hyper-alert senses. They can feel, hear, and see things that other people cannot. It is not that we see better; it is that we have better perception. Empaths are visionaries because they see everything from the outside while being present in the event. You probably consider things from various perspectives in an attempt to understand what is happening. Some people describe it as a bird's eye view—you see small details even in messy situations and with little information.

As a visionary, you often see the meaning in activities. Unfortunately, it is not always a beneficial thing because empaths tend to see only the good in people. Empaths doubt themselves when they see bad things in people— we want to believe everyone is good. You need to reign in your vision if you want to use it positively. Vision also makes it easy for you to identify people that are trying to manipulate you. Observe things from afar and question whether it is good or bad. Use your insights to effect change through visionary leadership. People will listen to you because they know that what you say is the truth and in their best interest.

Intuition

Empaths have a highly developed gut feel. Their intuition is stronger than anybody else's. Intuition helps in making decisions, especially when people are in a difficult situation. You know what the answers are to tough problems and easily make decisions, even when other people are still pondering their options. However, empaths tend to overthink things because we do not want to make the wrong decisions. When you doubt yourself, you question your intuition and break down your self-esteem. Stop doubting yourself.

Use your intuition for good things. Tell your friends when you have a bad feeling about someone's new partner. Trust your gut feel when it tells you someone is stuck or needs help. Use your intuition to guide yourself and those around you. As you empower your intuitive abilities, you become more self-confident and trusting. It gives you the power to control things within your abilities and alerts you to issues beyond your control.

Presence

Being with people is a strength of empaths. They have a keen sense of spatial awareness and know when people enter or exit a room. Other people pay attention when you walk into a room. Empaths are great at just being there. Yet, empaths shy away from social events because they know that the amount of energy is overwhelming.

Empaths can only use their presence when they start to accept themselves. Love yourself without limits. You are worthy of your talents but do not need to use them all the time. Other people know you are present without you imposing yourself. Allow your friends and family members to be themselves without interference. You do not have to take on the pain of other people and cannot control everything. Just be there–your presence will speak for itself.

Healing

Empaths are a plaster for the soul. People approach you with their problems and feel a weight lift off them after speaking to you. Empaths make things better. But, empaths often take on the wounds of those around them. You cannot keep doing this. It creates feelings of guilt and brings you down. It might even make you physically sick.

Only you can heal your wounds. Start the healing process by forgiving yourself and accepting your abilities. Do not self-sabotage. Be there for your friends but do not take on all their emotions. Try to shield yourself and control your own emotions. Take a breather often and meditate to refresh your energy. Once you have inner healing, you can start helping others who are hurting.

Creativity

All empaths are creative. They are artistic, have an eye for detail, and can add a flourish with ease. Empaths often enjoy movement activities and making things. Music soothes the soul and they see the beauty in all things. Yet, empaths struggle with personal expression. We worry about what people will say when we are our true selves.

Creativity is an outlet for emotion. Empaths carry around lots of emotion so use your creativity to quiet your soul. Artistic ability and free-thinking make it easy for you to make a difference. Be confident in your creative abilities. Start a book club, be an entrepreneur, or teach others to connect with their inner beings. Do not suppress your creativity. Rather, embrace it and let it bloom.

Set Up The Playing Field

Empaths can be emotionally strong or weak. Ultimately, you want to use your abilities and become mentally strong. Yet, empaths struggle with two things that decrease emotional resilience: wounds and communication.

Empaths have deep issues that stunt their mental strength. They take on other people's pain as if it is their own, then feel bad about it and harm their own emotions. Hurting because of others happens when you have poorly defined boundaries. You should not let yourself get hurt intentionally through other people's lives.

The other issue is that empaths are not great communicators. We hold our emotions to ourselves. Other people do not know how you feel and they cannot sense emotions as you do. You need to speak up about your feelings. Express yourself verbally and not just creatively. Start using clear language and tell people how you feel. It boosts your confidence and decreases the chance of misunderstandings.

Create Boundaries

Protecting your emotional space is important. Boundaries help you identify the non-negotiable behaviors in your life. Empaths need boundaries for all aspects of life, including emotions, energy, time, personal space, and ethics. Upholding boundaries allows you to have better relationships, which boosts your self-esteem because you know the other person is also happy. Setting boundaries protects you and allows you to conserve time and energy. You do not worry about things outside of your boundaries.

Boundaries require thought and intuition. Start by thinking about your rights and values. Your gut feel will bring up many of the ideas. One boundary could be to not feel guilty when saying no to someone. Another could be to treat others how you want to be treated–it will give a clear indication of when behavior is unacceptable. One important boundary is to acknowledge your shortcomings but not dwell on them. You are good enough!

Some flexible boundaries are possible. It depends on the person or situation, which makes you responsible for your own actions. Boundaries may change as you grow emotionally, but you can still be vulnerable. Crossing a boundary might cause temporary pain, but you learn from those experiences and fix the barrier. Think of your boundaries as a traffic light system. Give a green light if the activity agrees with you completely. A yellow light is when you start feeling uncomfortable about the boundary. A red light occurs when your intuition kicks in and you know that a boundary cannot be crossed at any cost.

Negotiate Friendships and Relationships

Empaths value friendships and relationships. It is not easy to have social interactions, but empaths can have flourishing friendships. Your boundaries are important to navigate relationships. A solid set of boundaries makes it easier for you to interact with other people and to identify inappropriate behavior. Remember that your family members and friends also have boundaries. Their ideas might not be the same as yours and that is okay.

It is our responsibility to respect each other's boundaries. You have cues when someone crosses your boundaries. Empaths might withdraw from a situation, or you might say, "I am uncomfortable." Either way, you will have your own methods to remove yourself from the event that is crossing your boundaries.

Protecting your privacy is important, so check that your journals have locks. Passwords protect your electronic devices and ensure you have a safe space at home that others will not enter. The people around you will have similar ways to protect their boundaries.

Successful relationships occur when we pick up on social cues and understand other people's boundaries. Most people give an indication when they feel uncomfortable or when you are crossing one of their boundaries. They might avoid eye contact, turn their body away from you, or fold their arms across their chest. Any body movement that seems protective or closed off is an indicator of unsettled boundaries. Some people will not respond or talk as much, and others might even flinch at the thought of the conversation. Be alert to these types of behaviors and stop the conversation immediately. Ask what your friend would rather do, or remove yourself from the situation for a few minutes. Asking questions is an excellent way to maintain boundaries, like asking your friend if you can give a hug when they are sad, rather than just approaching them. Mutual respect strengthens your relationships.

A Lifestyle

The way empaths live can be described as a lifestyle. You live, breathe, and interact differently than other people do. The routine, beliefs, and intuition of empaths make them live in a unique way, which enables them to contribute to the lives of others. An empath's lifestyle relies on managing energy and using your intuition in all actions.

Maintaining Energy

Empaths have a natural positive energy. Yet, this energy is volatile and becomes negative quickly if we take on the world's problems. Unfortunately, empaths have turbulent energy levels because we deal with so many emotions, interactions, and thoughts every minute. There is no rest at any time for empaths, so you must make a conscious decision to take a break. Restoring your energy after troublesome events is very important if you want to maintain a positive and energetic empath lifestyle.

Sleeping is a mission for empaths. You might have insomnia, sleep poorly, wake up frequently, and feel drained in the morning. Sharing the bed or room with another person can worsen your restlessness because of your affinity to emotions. Yet, sleep is a crucial source of mental and physical energy. It gives us time to rest, release hormones, and detoxicate. So, have a set bedtime routine that starts with positive energy by making a list of your achievements for that day. Even if you had a bad day, find one positive thing in it and focus your energy on it. This strategy helps to clear your mind before bed and gives a clean energy canvas. It makes it easier to wake up refreshed the next morning. If you had a bad night's sleep, then meditate, plan your day, and eat clean to regain neutral energy.

Energy is contagious. You catch it from those around you and share it wherever you go. Energy requires boundaries if you want to stay happy. Do not let things out of your control affect you negatively. It only decreases your energy while there is nothing you can do about it. Understand your limitations and place uncontrollable issues into the hands of the universe. Life will sort out itself. Smile and be optimistic. Be a light to everyone you touch through a positive mindset and willingness to make a difference. Positive energy requires work but it can become a natural occurrence in your life.

Trusting Your Intuition

Intuition, or gut feel, is a constant companion for empaths. It is a compass that guides your footsteps and decisions. Overthinking and our emotions sometimes cloud our judgment and silence our intuition. Another barrier to using intuition is the "what ifs" or "shoulds." What if I listen to my gut and someone gets hurt? Should I make another commitment to get someone's approval? No! Stop doing these things! Do not ignore your gut feel because of insecurities or wanting another person's approval. Rather ask yourself how a certain behavior will make you feel, so that you trust your intuition and maintain boundaries.

Pay attention to your intuition. You may notice it only in difficult or exciting situations, but gut feel is something that you can become more aware of. Self-awareness is crucial for intuitive decision-making. Bring your gut feel to the forefront by slowing down. Take a few deep breaths and clear your mind of other thoughts. You might place the situation at the back of your mind, but do not let it dominate your thoughts. Rather, focus on what your gut is telling you. Is it positive or negative? Does your intuition have a recommended course of action?

Intuition often displays itself as physical sensations. Pain on your stomach might indicate uneasiness in a social setting. Tingling in your fingertips and butterflies in your tummy signify excitement. There are so many small sensations in the body triggered by emotions and your gut feel. Empaths that slow down are open to physical sensations. One way to become more aware of your intuitive response is to name the emotion that you are feeling at that moment. Where do you feel the emotion? You might say the emotion is stress and feel it in tight shoulders. Focusing on the physical manifestation of your intuition enables you to be objective and make better decisions.

Many empaths feel intuition strongly but do not know how to use it. The previous strategies are methods that enhance awareness of your intuition and help to listen to it. Now you need to use it for positivity. Your intuition prompts your decision-making. It steers you in a certain direction, but many empaths doubt if it is correct. So, take your gut feel and question yourself about it. Will this decision harm others? Will it cross my boundaries or another person's boundaries? What good can this decision do? Asking yourself these questions will help you decide if your gut feel is correct. It might even make you realize that it is absolutely the best decision. Be aware of your body and soul, trust your gut feel, and thrive through positivity!

Conclusion

"Empaths did not come into this world to be victims, we came to be warriors. Be brave. Stay strong. We need all hands on deck." - Anthon St. Maarten

An invisible line connects empaths across the world. It is a cord made from the world's pain and interwoven with a strong motivation to fix universal issues. The line is important because empaths know the role they play in society. You might doubt your impact at the moment, but the lessons in this book can help you live to your full potential as an empath. You can grow! So, next time you feel alone as an empath, think of all the great empaths out there: Nelson Mandela, Hilary Swank, Mahatma Gandhi... and you!

Being an empath can be difficult. There are different types of empaths, each with their special talents. Some attract people, while others attune more to nature. Emotions become overwhelming and might get the better of you at times. Some empaths are very anxious and suffer bouts of depression. Hyperactive mirror neurons, contagious emotions, and biological sensitives all support the experiences of empaths. Luckily, structure, emotional awareness, expression, and boundaries help empaths to function positively. It is time to embrace your empath personality.

Emotional intelligence, resilience and mental strength all contribute to an empath's life. Empaths are acutely self-aware and have great social awareness, which draws people to them. However, empaths struggle with self-management and relationship management. Communication is not always a strong point, especially when empaths fear they are going to hurt someone else. Build your emotional resilience through personal, social, and life skills. Be assertive, remain positive and objective, and take time out for your own emotional wellbeing. Create healthy habits that improve your mental health, like setting goals and maintaining routines. Do not fear failure or risks. Rather, learn from your mistakes and take responsibility for your actions.

Friendships are synonymous with empaths. Everyone wants to be your friend, and you want to help other people. Yet, empaths only have a few close friends because not all people understand the depth of care that an empath has to give. Sometimes, empaths push friends away because they try to fix them rather than just giving mutual support. Unfortunately, some of your friends also try to manipulate you or use you as an emotional punching bag. Be very careful with these types of friendships. They will bring you down. It is better to have a small number of close friends that respect your boundaries and understand the blessing you are in their lives.

Intense romantic relationships are a priority in an empath's life. They give their entire heart to their partner, care deeply, and remain true to one person. An empath's romance is honest but you may not always communicate well. Tell your partner what you want and make compromises. It is absolutely fine to spend some time apart from each other or even to sleep separately. Just make sure you explain the situation to your partner, so that they understand that you are not pushing them away. You simply need time for recharging and sorting out your mind. A good partner understands these unique empath traits and will support you in all your endeavors. When things get tough, remember to stay in the moment and think about why your relationship is special. Do fun activities together, celebrate, and open yourself to each other's love.

Empaths have a myriad of career options. A job that suits your empathic characteristics allows you to flourish and gives the opportunity to enact major changes in society. Empaths often select creative or entrepreneurial careers in a variety of fields, from activism to teaching. Selecting a vocation must be done carefully so that you do not get hurt in the work process. Some jobs require tough decisions that you may perceive to hurt a living organism. Decide carefully whether this career aligns with your beliefs, or whether an alternate job is a better choice. Create a productive workspace for yourself and keep a schedule of goals and tasks. Maintain strict professional boundaries, do not engage in office gossip, and minimize time with energy-draining employees. Empaths often inspire colleagues through their positivity and collaborative leadership. Your career should make you happy and motivate you to get out of bed each day.

Every person's life has its own route. You cannot predetermine what will happen to you or anybody else. Life has times of mental growth and mental decline. Our emotions run rampant on this roller coaster. Empaths also become participants on the life roller coasters of friends, family members, and even strangers.

It is in your nature to want to help or even fix others. But, you cannot control everything. You are not responsible for the things that other people experience. Creating solid boundaries assists in navigating relationships and helps determine what type of assistance a person requires. Empaths can provide emotional or practical support. Simply keeping someone company already goes a long way. Do not overexert yourself and take time out to reflect on your emotions after challenging times. There is always a light at the end of the tunnel, so focus on that flickering of joy.

Empaths are blessed with special talents. The gifts of vision, intuition, presence, healing, and creativity are not given to just anybody. You were chosen to live with these talents. Each of these gifts plays a role in your life and together they make you a strong, independent superhuman. Use these gifts to touch others but also to make boundaries in your life. Set up a playing field that improves your life while making a difference in a greater context. Your team consists of many people, so treat each person with dignity and respect. You do not need to exhibit your talents to every person you meet. Rather, exhibit your gifts only to the most worthy players in your life–those who need your powers the most. Ensure that mutual respect exists in all your relationships so that boundaries do not blur. Be alert to social cues, maintain positive energy, trust your intuition, and stop doubting yourself.

Empaths experience great joy but also great suffering. As with all things, we must learn to accept the bad with the good. Better yet, we can come to appreciate the suffering, which can lead to growth and change. We can manage to find the light in every negative situation. It might hurt and it may take a long time to work through our emotions. But, after a while, you understand your emotions and the event. You realize your mistakes, or simply reflect on the unfairness of the world. These interactions build your mental strength. It makes you stronger emotionally and physically. You have the energy to face the world again. Now, as you face the world with your new, renewed strength–and more wisdom than you had before–you find yourself feeling serene. You find yourself feeling happy.

Acknowledge that…

I make mistakes but learn from them.

I am emotionally sensitive, yet I am strong.

I struggle at times but I overcome adversity.

I cannot fix other people.

I feel deeply but I am not responsible for other people's emotions.

I can maintain boundaries without feelings of guilt.

I persevere through self-care and intuitive abilities.

I am joy, peace, and an inspiration.

I am an empath.

References

Alder, S. L. (n.d.). "Sensitive people care…" quote. Goodreads. https://www.goodreads.com/quotes/tag/empaths

Bradberry, T. (2015, August 25). 15 Critical habits of mentally strong people. Forbes. https://www.forbes.com/sites/travisbradberry/2015/08/25/15-critical-habits-of-mentally-strong-people/#53b7d07e717b

Fon, R. (2018, July 26). 5 Experiences in life every empath goes through. IheartIntelligence. https://iheartintelligence.com/experiences-life-empath/

Garis, M. G. (2020, January 8). There are 8 types of empaths and only 1 has to do with feeling the emotions of others. Well + Good. https://www.wellandgood.com/types-of-empaths/

Harvard Professional Development. (2019, August 26). How to improve your emotional intelligence. https://blog.dce.harvard.edu/professional-development/how-improve-your-emotional-intelligence

Hurst, K. (n.d.). What are empaths? 14 Empath traits and scientific theories. The Law of Attraction.

https://www.thelawofattraction.com/empath-traits/

Kathrine, D. (2019, April 19). The reason this one thing is so important for an empath. Empaths Empowered. https://theknowing1.wordpress.com/tag/meditation-techniques/

Krznaric, R. (2010, March 27). The empathy top five: Who are the greatest empathists of all time? Outrospection. https://www.romankrznaric.com/outrospection/2010/03/27/407

Mascarelli, A. (2017). Find your meditation style with these 7 practices. Yoga Journal. https://www.yogajournal.com/meditation/find-meditation-style

Nollan, J. (2019, September 13). How to help others in their hour of need. A Conscious Rethink. https://www.aconsciousrethink.com/7410/help-others/

Pai, D. (2019, October 25). How to thrive at work as an empath. The M Dash. https://mmlafleur.com/mdash/thrive-at-work-empath

Parker, M. (2020, July 10). This is why empaths are the best people to be friends with. HerWay. https://herway.net/psychology/personality-types/empaths-best-people-friends/

Parpworth-Reynolds, C. (n.d.). Best careers for each type of empath. Subconscious Servant. https://subconsciousservant.com/best-careers-empaths/

Raypole, C. (2019). 30 Grounding techniques to quiet distressing thoughts. HealthLine. https://www.healthline.com/health/grounding-techniques

Sparacino, B. (2019, November 18). Empaths - Everything you need to know about this personality type. Thought Catalog. https://thoughtcatalog.com/bianca-sparacino/2018/05/empaths-everything-you-need-to-know-about-this-personality-type/

Spiegelman, M. (n.d.). 4 Must-have daily routines for the empowered empath. Beacons of Change. https://www.beaconsofchange.com/empowered-empath/

Spiegelman, M. (n.d.). 10 Resources for managing COVID-10 lockdown/ reopen reality. Beacons of Change. https://www.beaconsofchange.com/10-resources-for-managing-covid-19/

St. Maarten, A. "Empaths did not…" quote. Goodreads. https://www.goodreads.com/quotes/tag/empaths